Reflections
CLASS   ACC.

Heil Ruth
(LAST NAME OF AUTHOR)

My Child WITHIN — A young mother's reflections on becoming pregnant, being pregnant and giving birth.
(BOOK TITLE)

Crisis Pregnancy Center, Inc.
STAMP LIBRARY OWNERSHIP

CODE 4386-03   BROADMAN SUPPLIES
CLS-3   MADE IN U.S.A.

My Child Within

Ruth Heil

Crossway Books • Westchester, Illinois
A Division of Good News Publishers

My Child Within. *Copyright © 1983 by Ruth Heil.
Published by Crossway Books, a division of Good
News Publishers, Westchester, Illinois 60153.*

*All rights reserved. No part of this publication
may be reproduced, stored in a retrieval system or
transmitted in any form by any means, electronic,
mechanical, photocopy, recording, or otherwise,
without the prior permission of the publisher,
except as provided by USA copyright law.*

*Cover photo by: Four by Five.
Calligraphy by: Tim Botts.*

First printing, 1983.

Printed in the United States of America.

Library of Congress Catalog Card Number 82-83901.

ISBN 0-89107-268-3.

Contents

Foreword *by Ingrid Trobisch*   7

Chapter One   11
Chapter Two   30
Chapter Three   45
Chapter Four   60
Chapter Five   85

Foreword

I first met Ruth Heil when she was seventeen years old. She came into our family to help me take care of my own five small children before going on to nursing school. In our house she met her future husband, who was then still at seminary.

At that time Ruth was with us in order to learn. But now, through reading her book, I was able to learn from her and was richly blessed. I find three important messages in her book on motherhood:

First of all, becoming a mother is a process of growth. The reader gains this insight by traveling from page to page with Ruth Heil, and experiencing her gradual growth into the role of mother.

"Gradually I am learning to distinguish the important from the unimportant," she says. "And new sources of strength are opening up." Only when the mother has completely accepted herself as mother, and consequently can accept her child completely, do these sources of strength open up. And without them the mother will not be able to overcome the difficult situations in which she inevitably finds herself.

The second moving message of this book is that becoming a mother definitely does not mean being confined or being put into storage. On the contrary, it is an enormous opportunity for self-realization.

"It was an escape from the ghetto of duties which I had imposed on myself," says Ruth Heil. If you can share her amazement and joy at the discovery that a mother of five children can still find time to learn to play the flute, you will have grasped the message of this book.

However, I think the deepest lesson of *My Child Within* is a new insight into Jesus' words: "And whoever receives one such child in my name receives me" (Matthew 18:5)

That means nothing less than that God himself wants to encounter us in every child.

Many people would like to accept this gift of meeting God and God's joy in a child, but shrink from the task which comes with it. For that reason they reject the gift.

Ruth admits that she struggled with this temptation: "I am ashamed of myself; I want the gift called 'child' which brings me joy, without the task called 'child' which brings me work." But after facing the task, she can say, "What a sense of self-understanding

I am gaining from my children as I help them discover who they are."

With this sentence, Ruth Heil again touches on that joyful secret: God wants to meet us in the child. That's why it isn't only children who find themselves in relation to their mothers, but the other way around: mothers also find themselves as they encounter their children—they find their place in God's plan.

Ingrid Trobisch

Chapter One

It's early in the morning, and I am lying in bed. The children have left their small, warm sleeping-burrows in order to climb in and snuggle up next to me. I feel the little fingers glide carefully, lovingly over my sleepy face. They lie next to me, on top of me, each trying to squeeze as close as possible. I could shout for joy like a child. Who is desired as I am?

I kiss them one by one, take them into my arms, and laugh at them when their jealousy is awakened. Each suddenly believes himself to be shortchanged, and a great quarrel begins. A pillowfight ensues, and somersaults, and finally I get up.

You affluent people, just let yourselves be awakened by your programmed alarm clocks; enjoy your sleep in your elegant, clean beds. You are sleeping through all the delight of a fulfilled, rich life. You are robbing yourselves of the heaven on earth which makes all the drudgery, troubles, and concerns worthwhile. Feel sorry for me, you uninformed people, because of my work; I will pity you for your loss!

My journey to this heaven on earth began in the springtime, a few months after my twenty-first birthday.

May 5
Today the doctor confirmed it for me: I am expecting a child. A child—no, *our* child—is on the way! I am happy beyond words. I can hardly wait to tell Hans. A child is already living and growing inside me! All the May gardens bloom with beautiful colors—and inside of me lies the most precious and delicate bud of all. Soon I will be permitted to admire it, touch it, love it! I feel as if I could float home on a great flood of joy.

June 23
Apparently pregnancy is not all joy, even when you are looking forward to having the child. I'm only working half-days at the hospital now, but when I get up in the morning I'm already sick. Everything seems to upset my stomach, especially certain offensive odors. Today I just barely made it out of a patient's room before throwing up.

And the attitude of Mrs. K. continually upsets me. She always worries that I'm not taking care of her

Chapter One

well enough, even though I take special pains to please her. This morning when I brought her breakfast in, she thought her egg was too hard-boiled, the coffee was too watery, and there wasn't enough milk for her taste. I abruptly grabbed the tray and left the room. She complained so loudly that I refused to go back in the room all day, and I asked another nurse to take care of her.

I don't even recognize myself. Where has all my patience and my kindness gone? I plague myself with reproaches, but I can't find the strength to act differently. What kind of person am I, anyway, that I can't be longsuffering with sick people?

Sometimes even little things at home make me despair. The other day, the laundry basket full of clothes to be ironed looked like Mount Everest to me. I sat down in front of it and cried. Hans hurried into the kitchen to find out what the matter was. When I told him, he seemed reassured, and *that* upset me all over again. I'm noticing that he doesn't understand me. It bothers me that he sees my big problems as very small and trivial.

This evening, thinking it all over again, I find my behavior ridiculous. I don't understand myself.

August 16
For four months now I've been carrying this little miracle inside me. It must be about 6½ inches long by now. I'm sharply aware of its presence, even though I

can't see it or feel it. It accompanies me day and night. It influences both dream and reality.

Old images from the past haunt me: An operating room, an anesthetized woman, the opened abdominal cavity, the four-month-old fetus in the amniotic sack, its uncontrolled movements. The sack is ruptured, the umbilical cord clamped; we watch a few final convulsions in the tiny figure—desperate movements from a powerless person helpless to defend himself.

Then I am called upon to carry the litte person away. I walk down the corridor, barely capable of holding on to the receptacle. I am completely dazed. I have witnessed the careful murder of a human being, and no detectives will come to investigate. A life was snuffed out, and no one is even mourning it.

The next day I take care of the woman who had the surgery. She feels relieved. She isn't married and she didn't want the child. Since she has a congenital heart defect, her abortion was, conveniently, medically sanctioned.

My child, I don't know whether I'll be able to offer you a good life. I don't know if I'll be able to give you everything I would like to give you. But I wholeheartedly want you; and I already love you.

August 25
I'm in my fifth month of pregnancy. Sometimes I'm torn between affection for the child and anger over my new situation. The morning sickness has let up, which

I see as a special blessing. But I have something new to deal with: my belly is getting so round! My secret isn't a secret anymore. This new, adult role is difficult for me to play. My body makes me feel so tied down, and it utterly excludes me from the ranks of the desirables. I'm inhibited around other people.

Is it possible that this time of isolation is developing a special bond between myself and the child within me?

I do believe it is important to resolve this battle of conflicting feelings, instead of just pushing it aside.

August 28
Amazed, I sit still and listen. Something has moved in me, something that was in me but not part of me. A boundless joy and satisfaction fill me, as I begin to comprehend that it is my child. I have the privilege of transmitting life!

A small person is slumbering inside me, now, this very hour. Does he experience my feelings along with me? Is he aware of my thinking, and my longing for his arrival? Four more months. Why does pregnancy have to last so long?

Despite the joy, I'm conscious of anxiety. I'm afraid of the unknown experience of giving birth, and I wonder how to fulfill my new task of motherhood. But the joy predominates, and it overcomes my worries. I think my most important calling right now is to listen to that good voice, and to always believe it.

September 20

Together Hans and I have read the book *Husband Coached Childbirth* by Robert A. Bradley (Harper & Row, 1981). Dr. Bradley says that the husband is very important during pregnancy. He should take an active part in all the preparations. Dr. Bradley describes animal births with great enthusiasm, pointing out how naturally it occurs with them. The doctor also gives practical advice—for instance, crawling through the apartment on all fours as a relaxation exercise for the spinal column. Hans insists that I do this exercise. But as "active participant" he himself must join in, of course. He slides through the legs of the kitchen chairs and under the table, crawling from the kitchen to the living room and into the bathroom, and always through tight spots or across obstacles. We laugh a lot, and these hours of hilarity do both of us good. Not only does the exercise, surprisingly, ease my lower backache, but it also brings about a relaxation of the tension between us. For I often feel that Hans doesn't understand me or take me seriously. I've become easily offended and resentful, traits ordinarily foreign to my personality. And I am usually moody. When Hans treats me affectionately, I want to be left alone; when he falls asleep next to me, I long to have a conversation.

Pregnancy upsets my equilibrium so much that sometimes I can't stand myself. So I rejoice in these hours together when we can relax and laugh while reading this book and doing the exercises.

Chapter One

October 9
My feelings of isolation are gradually letting up. Oddly enough, others seem to behave more positively toward me the further the pregnancy progresses. Or am I the one that is changing? In any case, I'm happy to return to our circle of friends.

And I am finding that small tokens of affection from others help me get through the hours of discomfort or depression. It was nice of Mrs. Becker in the grocery store to serve me first—and no one else was annoyed by her doing that. And someone told me that pregnancy had made me really lovely; the small compliment helps me to accept my physical state.

This morning the mailman brought me a package with no return address. I opened it with curiosity, and found a cute pair of rompers and a baby bib. A flowered card said, "For my grandchild," in my mother's handwriting. I smile; would she prefer a boy? At any rate, I appreciate her great joy.

October 18—A Letter to My Unborn Child
My beloved child,

I do not know you yet. Only the movement in my body which is not part of me reminds me of your existence, over and over. But I already love you with my whole heart—not just because you are *my* child, but because you are the child of him who is closer to me than anyone else on earth.

Many new experiences await you, and us. You

are our first! Right now, you live in a sheltered, unconscious world. No one requires anything of you; you are still safe. But we, your parents, await your coming with joy. Sometimes I am afraid of that strange, new moment when I will first hold you in my arms. There will be plenty of nights when your crying will irritate us. And there will be days when you are annoyed with us, or unhappy because we don't understand you. The day will come when you will leave us, and we you.

But we will always belong to one another. We will remain in communion because you are a part of us—a visible sign of your parents' unity. We know that you are God's gift to us!

October 30
We are moving to a larger apartment. It's very hard for me to say good-bye to "my" hospital. I had a good rapport with many people there, especially those patients who have been ill for a long time. All of my impatient feelings about their behavior have disappeared. I find myself especially sympathetic towards sick people. Peculiar, the strong fluctuations in mood a pregnancy brings about! I'm very happy to be liberated from the impatient phase which depressed me so much. I feel well physically, too.

After we move, I will not start another job. I need to gather strength for my new task of being a mother.

Chapter One

November 10

I want Hans to be present at the birth. And he would like to be there. But sometimes I am overcome by a fear of failing, of not being able to control myself. I don't want him to see me in such a miserable state. I have seen about fifty deliveries as a nurse. The process of birth always fascinates me—but I also remember those hours in which women rolled around helplessly with their labor pains. The few husbands who stayed around usually waited in a lobby. They hid their anxiety, somewhat imperfectly, behind large newspapers; I remember one man who held his newspaper upside-down! When I came out of the delivery room, they would shove those large papers aside, looking at me so expectantly, so full of hope.

Is it right to exclude the husband? Isn't it better to let him take part? Perhaps the man who is becoming a father should experience this hour of failure, of fear, of the "hospital atmosphere" firsthand. More importantly, perhaps he deserves to witness the great moment in which a new life is born into the world. I think of the joyful light that shines from the eyes of a new mother. I have been kissed and embraced by strangers; once a mother pressed my arm so hard in pure joy that it hurt for days afterward. This participation was not rightly mine. I received something which belonged to the women's own husbands.

Often I think of Mary; I have carefully reread the Christmas story in the Gospel of Luke. In those days it was customary to have relatives present at a child's birth, and also midwives who were usually married women. I made an astonishing discovery which almost takes my breath away: Mary and Joseph were in a stable in Bethlehem, far away from all activity. And there in the stable Joseph must have been the "midwife." For it says of Mary that "she (singular) wrapped him in cloths, and laid him in a manger" (Luke 2:7).

No one was there to help: The shepherds, who had been the first to hear the happy news, found only Mary and Joseph and the child in the manger (Luke 2:16). In the midst of a noisy, busy night, two people who loved each other went through the depths together, and together they experienced the wonderful arrival of the child. Maybe it was exactly because of these hours that Mary's husband was given such a close relation to Jesus that he was able to stand with Jesus as a father.

Yes, my husband has to be present at the birth of our child! I want us to experience these moments together.

November 29
Yesterday we went to another prenatal examination.

"So you would like your husband to be present at the delivery?"

"Yes."

"And are you aware of what he will have to endure there? He'll see you suffer, and he won't be able to help. He may faint when he sees blood—then we'd have to take care of him too. Or he might get too excited, and get in the way." The physician looked at me doubtfully.

I answered, "It will make me happy to have my husband with me in those hours—and he wants to be there too. If you don't think you can be accountable for this, we'll have our child in a different hospital."

The doctor burst out laughing. "Well, so you want to have the child together? By all means, come. I hope you'll let me come, too—I intend to take part in this delivery!"

Now that I know Hans will be with me, I'm preparing for the birth as for an exam. I have renewed enthusiasm for my gymnastic exercises; I want to do all I can to make it a good experience for us both.

December 5

Soon I will be in my ninth month. Our little one has grown so much that stooping is difficult for me, and I can't climb stairs as energetically as I used to.

The baby is relatively quiet during the day, but he seems to enjoy making his presence known at night. I hope he doesn't cry like that later!

In the evenings our little darling gets lots of kisses from his Daddy—on my belly. Sometimes I'm almost forgotten in the process, and I have to complain: after all, I do have first rights!

We have calculated January 10 for his arrival. I

wonder whether he'll act according to our calendar, or prefer his own.

December 14

I am in the hospital. On Thursday my water broke prematurely, and Hans hurriedly brought me to the hospital. Since my water is broken, they're not giving me any medication to induce labor; instead they want to prolong the birth as much as possible, since the due date isn't for another four weeks. Of course Hans can't be with me all the time, but they have promised to call him as soon as the contractions start coming at shorter intervals. I'm happy that they're letting Hans be present at the birth.

December 15

This room is dimly lit, for which I am thankful. Nevertheless, I feel thoroughly miserable. I've been having labor pains for two days and two nights already. I admit they're still bearable; but they make it hard to sleep. And they won't let me get up, either. Since the child has moved even deeper into my pelvic area, I feel a constant urge to go to the bathroom. But I don't dare call the night nurse, for fear she will be annoyed. She comes in with such an unfriendly expression on her face, shoves the bedpan under me, and disappears again. I don't even know her name. She hasn't spoken a word to me yet. Now and then she examines me, mumbles something inaudible, and leaves again. I'm longing for a single encouraging word, or even a human sound. I keep picturing Hans, lying in his nice warm bed at home, sleeping.

December 16
You're here: You little human being! Our dear Mark! I've already rocked you in my arms, and I had to restrain myself from squeezing you too tightly out of joy. You're such a little darling, with your dark tuft of hair and your blue eyes. I don't get to see those precious eyes very often, because your eyelids are still so heavy, and opening them takes so much energy. But you often grab my finger and hold it as if you never want to let it go. Today you pulled my finger to your tiny mouth, which resembles your father's, and you gnawed on it reproachfully. Just be patient, my little one—soon I'll be able to nurse you!

I heard your first cry shortly after midnight. I saw you as a little blue Something, hanging on the umbilical cord between the doctor's hands. Your father was there; he comforted me wonderfully throughout your birth, holding my hand in both of his. You weigh almost 6½ pounds. But during the delivery I thought you must weigh at least 100! It was not as simple as I thought it would be. I was so weak from the previous nights that I had very little strength with which to push. And everything dragged out even longer because it was a breech birth. By the time the delivery was over, I was totally exhausted—but also boundlessly happy.

December 20

I'm in a double room. My roommate gave birth before I did, and she nurses her child easily and matter-of-factly. It's not working out so smoothly for me. By the time Mark finally starts to drink, the nurse is already taking him away again to be weighed. This upsets me, because he never gets enough. My roommate's baby regularly drinks *more* than he is expected to. I feel as if I'm under pressure to perform. I break down and cry at small things, and I hate it but I can't stop.

But whenever they bring my child in, all the tension inside me evaporates. Even if I can't give him enough milk, there is plenty of love. When I hold my little one and he looks at me, I see myself in his features. I encounter a part of my own being in him—here is a part of myself that I can love unrestrictedly, without being egoistic. I'm finding a path to myself by coming near to my child. I'm achieving some self-acceptance, and learning to rejoice in my existence because of his existence. I want to pour myself out in exultant praise for the gift of being human!

December 22

I am still in the hospital, but tomorrow Hans will come to take us home. Now we're a real family. I'm looking forward to having our little intruder with me all the time, but I'm afraid too. Will I do everything right?

Chapter One

December 23
We're home! Hans has cut out a large newspaper ad and hung it on the door: A sparrow sits on the roof of a house, and the caption says, "A little bird is telling everyone: 'We have a son!'" In the living room, I find a vase filled with large pine branches—of course, it's Christmas! I am appreciating the wonder of the Incarnation more than ever before. How helplessly he came to earth, the King of kings, becoming poor that we might become rich!

I tuck my own tiny, fragile Mark into his crib. As a nurse, I've taken care of plenty of small children and babies—but taking care of my own is another matter. Thank goodness Hans is here.

December 24
Well, we've survived our first night as a family. And I'm lying in bed, totally exhausted. What a giant-sized voice lives in that tiny body! I remember this night as a confused mixture of cold (our landlord turned down the heat), hot (nursing makes me so weak that sweat runs down my body), and, most of all, screaming: Whenever we fell asleep, Mark began to cry again. Since he was premature, he's too weak to nurse well. He gets worn-out while drinking, falls asleep, is soon hungry again, wakes up, cries....

December 30

Do children bring more joy or more trouble? At this point, I'm not sure. To begin with, the washing machine broke down today, and I had to do all the laundry by hand. Then I tried to nurse Mark, and hardly any milk would come. I don't like nursing anyway—it certainly doesn't bring me the feelings of joy and fulfillment that Ingrid Trobisch told me it would. It's uncomfortable, and I can't even find the right position. Lying down doesn't work, and sitting up is terribly tiring. I find the procedure most bearable in my rocking chair. I'm definitely only doing it for the sake of the child.

January 20

I am at my wit's end. So is Hans. Our complete helplessness makes us angry at one another, and I keep having to bite my tongue to avoid yelling at him. I want to blame my husband for all the baby's screaming—but that's so unfair.

Last night we shoved the little screamer into the living room, hoping we could ignore his "music." But whenever he quieted down, I was afraid he might have vomited or stopped breathing. So I would get up to check on him, wake him by opening and closing the door—and the concert would start up all over again. How do other parents stand it? And what if they have two or three children? All day long I feed, change diapers, cook and iron; and the nights seem eternal.

Chapter One

My twenty-second birthday is five days away. I can't help but recall my happy twenty-first birthday. Hans gave me a carrot cake: a great gift of love from him, since he doesn't like it. I lay on my bed, surrounded by the aroma of our afternoon coffee and flowers from many friends, and I looked at my sleeping husband. I asked myself why I wasn't completely happy. We had been married over a year, and still there was no sign of a child. Before our wedding, we had agreed that we wanted lots of children. A child, I thought, is an unbuyable gift; and I prayed to God that he would entrust us with that treasure.

Looking back on that day makes me feel so old and worn-out.

January 27
Today Beatrice called me. She told me that every time her baby cries, and her husband sleeps peacefully on, it makes her furious. So sometimes, after feeding the child, she shines a flashlight into her husband's face until he wakes up! I fully understand her feelings; though it never occurred to me to waken Hans with a flashlight, I'm absolutely capable of doing something like that. My whole attitude toward life is colored by this little screaming bundle, this *intruder*. Mark makes his presence known during the best sleep, during the nicest conversation; and he's too loud and demanding to be ignored.

Hans is probably just as frustrated as I am. Even

my pregnancy was hard on him: my changed appearance, my moodiness, and my continual complaints. I need to have more concern for his feelings.

February 8
Mark is seven weeks old. I'm afraid that my milk doesn't give him proper nourishment—it looks blue and watery compared to cow's milk. At the infants' clinic they told me to start offering him a bottle. They also said that he doesn't weigh as much as he should, according to the charts. Maybe my poor child cries all the time because he's hungry? I won't mind cutting down on the nursing—all this continual rocking gets on my nerves.

February 22
I'm giving Mark a bottle, but he's not crying any less. We are getting used to it, though, and the pediatrician says he is healthy. The doctor explained that this "three-months-crying" occurs with many babies. My milk was decreased, and I only nurse Mark twice a day now. Although it's a relief, somehow I miss the five times a day. I can't quite put it into words . . . oh well, it can't be changed now.

March 10
Today my child's whole little face beamed at me like a bright, warm sun: The first smile! Conscious or unconscious—who cares? I feel like singing. This bliss

compensates for all those sleepless nights! I can't wait till Hans gets home.

March 14
Every day I discover something new about my child. The little person has become a true Other. He is happiest when he is very close to me; I carry him around on my arm. He already dislikes being alone. And I want him near me all the time: often I stand beside the crib and listen to the little sleeper's breathing. When he wakes up, I put him on the kitchen table in his infant seat and chat with him as I peel potatoes or write a letter.

And Hans is crazy about his son—when he comes home, he picks Mark up right away. He's already adept at changing diapers. But when he feeds the baby the food flies all over! Mark eats very quickly, and if the spoon doesn't reappear in time he complains loudly, spraying bits of carrots or spinach from his mouth all over our clothes, the table, and the floor.

We take long walks, with Mark in his baby carriage. He sleeps away most of his time in the beautiful outdoors, but the air does him good, and he is with us wherever we go.

I'm so glad to have those first three months behind me. Mark is sleeping through the night now, and I'm beginning to recover my strength. That period after the birth *was* a fulfilled time, in spite of all the difficulties. I can feel the sun's warmth as it shines through the window: Spring will come quickly now.

May 10 — Mother's Day
Dearest Mother,

Today is your day. It's unfair to appoint only one day in the year to praise mothers, for you are so precious that every day I give thanks for your existence. What a wonderful gift of God a mother is!

I have grown up, I've "flown the coop," but I'm still your child. We belong to each other, although we no longer live together. You've left your stamp on me, and your motherhood has led the way for mine.

One generation follows another. But in all the turmoil of history, one thing remains changeless: the image of the loving mother in the heart of her child. I think that, when that image is present, a nation is able to be strong and to bear hardships. When the image is lacking, the richest country becomes poor: fear grows, love dies, creative power is paralyzed. I think that a secure childhood is necessary in order to grow up and take on responsibility. Without it, life's disciplines become a burden. And, without it, one is unwilling to add to that load by allowing a child to be born into one's life. Because you, Mother, permitted me to really be a child, the demands of adulthood aren't a burden to me but a satisfying, challenging task. Because you love me so much, I am now also able to love.

What a special gift you are from God! My heartfelt thanks for all your sharing of my thoughts, my burdens, and my sorrows. I embrace you in love.

Your child

I've found a new, closer relationship with my mother. In the past we didn't get along very well; I imagined she favored my brothers and sisters. Sometimes I thought I hated her.

Today, everything looks different. Just think, my mother had already encountered all these problems and joys of motherhood, long before I even existed! I feel such an abundance of love for my parents, now. We don't get together very often, but we feel the ties strongly.

I understand now something of the joy and pain my parents went through in having children. In a way, the very act of birth was a surrendering of my child. The pain of the severed umbilical cord isn't physical, but nonetheless real. Never again will I be so closely connected to him; never again will he belong to me so directly. But the child must leave the womb in order to enter the world. We pay much for the joy of having children: we lose our personal freedom while being forced to give the child greater and greater independence. But I think our marriage will be deepened and enriched by the experience. And the joy will always be greater than the price to be paid.

May 24

Mark is five months old, and unspeakably precious to me. As I was dressing him today he softly touched my face. I saw his shining eyes. It was as if he said: *You are here. How good it is that you exist.* Mentally I answered: *You are here too. How good it is that you exist!*

How rich this little human being has made us! We're glad to be a family rather than just a married couple. Our lives no longer revolve only around *us*—two people living only for themselves. In these past few months, many friends came to share in our joy, and ended up sharing their burdens with us as well. Mark has made us better, more sympathetic listeners.

Chapter Two

May 27
Because of my nursing, the first ovulation came several weeks late. We didn't plan on a second child so soon, even though we wanted several children. But it's on its way.

I honestly don't think I can handle another child at this point. However, I'm once again excited over the profound experience of carrying a new life within. The immortal God uses me, a mortal being, to take part in creating another. He must see some great value in me, despite all my failings.

I'm not as dizzy and nauseated as I was in my pregnancy with Mark, and I fully appreciate that blessing. But again I suffer from up-and-down emotions. Poor Hans has trouble comprehending my moods. Today I fled to Mark's crib for consolation. Instead of sympathizing, my child pulled himself up by the bars, yanked my hair, and cheered loudly at my "ouch!" He lay down on his back in order to see my face. He stuck his hand in my mouth to feel my teeth. And whenever he got me to make a sound, he laughed with joy. Surprisingly, this treatment helped more than anything. It was like the little guy was asking, "You don't want something like me again, do you?" Yes, I do! Of course I do.

September 15
Such sharpness in my reactions nowadays! When Elisabeth called and talked about her problems, I had a hard time trying to be understanding. I really wasn't very nice to her. Again and again motherhood shows me the deep chasms of my being, and I am ashamed about what is hidden inside me.

Hans doesn't know what to do for me. He is kind, but sometimes I feel he doesn't pay proper attention to my important condition. Well, what do I expect? Hans does participate in the pregnancy in his own way: He doesn't crave pickles, but there's always something specific he wants, at some odd time of day or night! So yesterday evening at nine I showed up at our neighbors, asking to buy a bottle of beer. The neighbor handed it to me with a knowing smile . . . if only he'd known who it was really for!

I have my "up" moments too: I take great pleasure in being creative. What a wealth of deep capacity for experience! All the possibilities of my life, both depths and heights, seem to be exposed. If only the transitions between were smoother. First I am triumphant and flushed with the victory of my new achievement; then I'm plunged to the depths of despair; then, once more, I'm walking on air. I need to learn to master this deep capacity for feeling.

October 16
Mark will celebrate his first birthday in two months. And if our second child comes according to schedule, our son will have a new little brother or sister on his birthday. What better or more beautiful "toy" could we give him? What a gift to look forward to: unique and priceless. I talk to Mark all the time about his new brother or sister. He can't understand yet. But somehow he knows that it means something very wonderful, because he laughs with joy whenever I mention the baby. Does he sense my happiness? I expect a full measure of joy with this child; and I'm not afraid of all the work.

I read recently that pregnancy is the best time in a woman's life. It's definitely true. This experience changes me internally as well as externally; it makes me grow, and forces me to visit new horizons I'd never dreamed of. I do chafe at the physical limitations. I can hardly find a comfortable position for sleep. Climbing stairs makes me puff like a steam engine. And my shopping basket weighs a hundred pounds now! But probably everything that limits our environment and hinders our freedom of movement—even those very dear to us—seems to be a burden, at times.

November 18
Only three more weeks—I'm really looking forward to having this new child!

But I'm constantly oppressed by unreasonable fears: the baby will be born dead, or with some kind of deformity. The thought weighs on me, depressing my days and haunting my dreams at night. I try to shake it off, but it stays on my heels like a bloodhound.

And other fears sit heavily upon me. I wonder if Hans would marry again, if I died. I worry that a second wife would be unkind to our children. I even talked to Hans about this, and he took me into his arms and told me how much he loved me. It helped—but still I secretly imagine that he doesn't like me as much as he used to, and that he's *really* looking forward to marrying somebody else. I know that's not true... the truth is that I just can't stand myself with this belly. It interferes with all my movements, and I'm sick and tired of looking so awkward and shapless in these loose maternity clothes. I want to cover up all our mirrors. Thank God it's only three more weeks!

November 21
Today I received an upsetting letter. Monica, a close friend, says, "Pregnancy ruined all our plans. Bert and I were looking forward to some vacation trips together.

And I had just been accepted into the university when we found out that I was pregnant. First, we had to move into a larger apartment, far away from my parents. Then there was the continuous weight gains. All my life I've fought against fat, and in pregnancy it found its revenge.

"I did feel well, physically—no morning sickness. My arms and legs only started hurting in the very last nights before delivery; I would wake up and think they were about to fall off.

"But the delivery itself was a nightmare. To this day I haven't completely gotten over it. The beginning was bearable. But the doctor decided to induce labor by breaking my water, and after that the pains became horrible. The contractions came every two or three minutes, and each one lasted almost that long. It was terrible—partly because your account of delivery had given me such different expectations. Please don't take that as an accusation; I'm sure that it *was* the way you say it was, for you, and I'm happy for you.

"Bert stayed with me during the whole time, and sometimes I felt real hatred for him. It seemed so unfair that I had to endure all that pain, and he got off scot-free. When we got home, those hate feelings were transferred to Stephanie, because I felt so tied down. I only found joy in motherhood when Stephanie grew big enough for me to feel love from her.

"Now everything's going well, and the little one really brings sunshine into our lives. But if I'd known then what I know now, I would have prevented a pregnancy by any possible means. Or at least I wouldn't have allowed labor to be induced."

I feel that the delivery would have been easier if only Monica had made a more positive response to her pregnancy. Still, the letter makes me uneasy: have I forgotten all the pain of the first birth already? Has my memory whitewashed all the bad with optimism? Miserably, I waver between fear and hope. I try to recall details.

I remember the horror of the lonely hospital room during the dark hours of the night. Minutes crept along like hours. Every night, for three nights, they left me in there because they were expecting the delivery any time. They wouldn't let me get up, because my water had already broken. Each evening they sent Hans home, promising to call him when the labor pains got stronger. So I was left alone in the dark, waiting fearfully for the next contraction.

The hours which Hans spent with me are a much happier memory. He would sit by my bed and chat, and I could almost forget my backaches in the joy of those moments.

And even during the worst of the labor his presence was a great comfort to me. When I picture the delivery, I see only his loving face against a blurred background. He was with me, all the way. The more I think about it, the calmer I become: Hans will be with me. To the doctor, I'm a patient—one of many. But to my husband I am the only wife.

I feel comforted already.

November 29
And now a letter from my friend Cornelia. I remember her reproachful letter of a few weeks ago. She was expecting her second child in only a few days, and she wrote, "How can you talk about your delivery so cheerfully? I had a horrible experience, and I'm afraid of this second birth even though I want the child. You must be exaggerating a bit: My delivery not only tore external wounds into me, it also wore me down inwardly."

Now I can hear my heart beating as I rip the envelope open. Has she had her baby yet?

"Oh Ruth, didn't I write to you about the delivery? We had to drive to the hospital on a very snowy winter night, and Veronica was born within an hour. True, she came vehemently, but the whole experience was wonderful. Something deep inside me has been healed. Just driving past the hospital gives me a thrill of joy now! Of course Peter was present, too.

"At first nursing was harder than it had been before, when I gave birth at home. The hospital routine obviously isn't the best introduction. But my little Veronica and I have become a practiced pair. I'm so thankful that I can nurse her fully: It's the easiest way to do it when you're traveling, and the experience is such a joy in itself."

I breathe a sigh of relief. Apparently every birth

is different. And every birth gives us more understanding of how we are meant to treat our bodies.

November 30
I've covered the baby carriage in a friendly red and white checked material. I keep pushing it through the apartment, pretending that a little girl—my secret desire—lies in it. Hans saw me, and laughed. "You push that carriage as if it already held something." Well, it's true, my child, you exist, even though I can't yet hold you in my arms! I couldn't love you more than I already love you now.

December 7
Our Esther has been born! It all happened so fast that I can hardly comprehend how suddenly our family has increased.

Hans brought me to the clinic at five A.M. because I was bleeding lightly. The labor began around 8, and the contractions rapidly became so heavy that I tried to calls Hans at work. I kept dialing the wrong number, so by the time I reached him he was barely able to get here in time. Probably the labor proceeded with such speed because the birth-canal was still widened from my last delivery.

How wonderful to have my husband present for this birth, too! Whom else was I supposed to kiss when our little girl appeared? Who would have I hugged with joy, if he hadn't been there? And he *was* there, at the precise moment when our new little creation first manifested herself. It was unspeakably beautiful when she was called into life at conception, but a thousand times more so now that she had become a visible sign of our relationship.

The nurses have sent Hans home. They told me I needed to rest. Sleep? It's out of the question! It's Sunday morning, and the bells are ringing everywhere. I feel like I'm experiencing a bit of eternity. I'm at the high point of my life, and I want to enjoy these moments, drink my fill of them. I wish they would give me my child back—I want to hold her and share this joy with her. I'm dreaming with open eyes... dream? No, fabulous reality!

My beloved child, I'm so glad that you're a reality. You! You real, live human being: your little hands move, your soft velvet skin can be caressed, your two bright eyes gaze back at me, your mouth searches and cries for food. And everything healthy... what happy, dreamlike reality!

December 20
Mark looks at this new little bundle with astonishment. When I nurse the baby, he watches with wide-open eyes. He lays his head on my knee and becomes unusually quiet. I had such mixed emotions about nursing Esther—I kept remembering all the failure and discomfort of a year ago, and all my weak dissatisfaction with myself. But Esther drinks well, and my tension is

slowly evaporating. Probably I'm more relaxed about it this time.

I do worry that she's not getting enough. The nurse strongly advised me not to nurse the baby more than six times a day. Still, it interrupts my sleep, and Mark is so lively that he demands all my energy in the daytime. Today I lost track of him for a moment, and he ate some laundry detergent. I'm still shaken from that little incident. So when I tried to nurse Esther there was hardly any milk, and she cried and cried. Maybe I'd better start supplementing with the bottle.

March 10

Esther is already twelve weeks old! The other day I nursed her for the last time, and now she's getting all her milk from a bottle. I miss the nursing, and so does she; when I hold her in my arms, she snuggles up very close to me. Just think, her little heart grew and her limbs were formed inside my uterus for nine months, and suddenly she is a separate little person who can live without me. I feel like the door to a very deep understanding of things has slammed shut behind me. It's hard to put it into words. I have a longing for a lost paradise. I really wasn't any more thrilled about nursing this time, though it wasn't as tiring as nursing Mark. Maybe I just miss holding my little one so often, and talking to her. We each seem to understand what the other is saying.

Chapter Two

March 17
If only I had a stronger faith in the words of Psalm 127: "Children are a gift of the Lord; the fruit of the womb is a reward." This verse makes no mention of the demands and claims of children—but how often I feel this gift as a burden rather than the joy it should be!

Today I'm physically exhausted. Exactly five times I have undone dirty brown diapers and cleaned two baby bottoms—a never-ending, fruitless task, since it returns again and again. A gift? Sometimes the smell lingers on my hands all day. And just today someone asked me to design a birth announcement for her! I think of this particular friend's situation: She really didn't want the child in the first place. In a fit of inspiration I grab a pen and write:

"Children are a plague of the Lord; the fruit
of the womb is a special punishment.
We announce the birth of our first, unwanted child.
We anticipate all the exhaustion
we have to look forward to.
Both the parents
And the grandparents,
Also hard-hit,
Will take pains to prevent further children."

It makes me laugh, but I'm ashamed of myself. I want the gift called "child" which brings me joy without the task called "child" which brings me work. But you have to learn the care and usage of a gift before you recognize its value!

April 5

Spring has come again; yellow cowslips bloom along all the brooks. After the days of cold and darkness, nature puts on her wedding dress. I want to celebrate this wedding along with the creation. And spring symbolizes more than the wedding day—it's a picture of new birth. Only a few more labor pains, and new life, a new creation will become visible. The trees are still bare, but the meadows are covered with a soft fluff like the small, downy head of a newborn.

No tree or flower becomes uglier than in winter, when it dies so it can rewaken in spring. So too I enter a dark valley with every pregnancy, from which I emerge with a child, a new life; every child seems to bring a new springtime into my life.

Everyone rejoices in the awakening of nature. But how many people refuse to participate personally in the Creation! They won't integrate the message of springtime into their own lives. Or they're too indifferent to care that all becoming is an expression of our personal Creator. Whenever we take part in his work we see a bit of his greatness. But when comfort and pleasure dull the conscience, we have less concern for other people. Then the responsibilities of life start looking like burdens rather than joys.

Each child draws me further out of the prison of

self-centeredness. In the child, God himself meets me. Every birth seems like an encounter with God; I sense God's breath of life, and he seems close enough to reach out and touch. How miraculously I am connected to God: Not only did he give me life, but he allows me to transmit it to others! Every child deepens this incomprehensible experience—and reawakens a longing to have more children.

That longing is certainly present; but I'm learning to admit the limits of my energy. I realize now that two babies within a year is too much. My body needs a longer period of rest after pregnancy. Ingrid Trobisch's book *The Joy of Being a Woman* (Harper & Row, 1975), and other books on married love give us helpful advice on planning pregnancies. I think it's important for Esther to learn to walk before we have another child. The strain of taking care of two small babies would be too much for me.

But I'm glad that Mark has already accepted his little sister as a matter of course. The other day I found him in the nursery, standing by Esther's crib. He was reaching his hands through the bars, gently petting his little sister's head and saying "Aah ... aah," up and down the scale. How wonderful that he already loves her, and has no conception of jealousy.

June 24
A morning like any other. It took all my strength just to climb out of bed. I'm so tired, and it seems like the

night should have just started, but the sun is already high in the sky and shining brightly. It can't brighten my sleepy eyes much. I feel overworked, and drained. I'm cross to everyone I encounter, though I don't mean to be. Here it is 10 o'clock already, and I'm still running around in my bathrobe! Even getting washed and dressed seems a huge chore.

I used to be involved in so many things! Now that I don't even work outside the home anymore, I get nothing done. Resentment rises in me. Do I have to sacrifice *everything* for the sake of the children? Isn't it enough that I hardly get a decent night's sleep because of them? And I wanted these two little ones so badly. Perhaps the others were right—those others who didn't want children because it meant giving up their own comfort. Maybe I was crazy to view children as a joy. Maybe it was a confused, misunderstood yearning for my own childhood.

I must find the way out of this labyrinth of work. Something will have to change, because I can't stand life like this much longer.

July 5
I've just had a good experience. Yesterday I went to bed in spite of all the unfinished work. And this morning it was easier to do than usual. Apparently my body needs more rest. I need to be willing to leave even important tasks undone. My perfectionism is part of the reason why I never seem to finish my work. But if

I'm patient with myself, things will get easier. I just need to admit my limitations and learn to live with them.

It's been two weeks since the windows were washed: Unthinkable! But they really don't look so bad. Last window-washing afternoon I shirked my chores and took a long walk with the children instead. The weather was beautiful, and we gathered large bunches of brightly colored wildflowers. To my surprise I found myself humming a song. I felt so light and free, as if a leash had been loosed or chains had fallen away from me. The children's laughter sounded like lovely music to me. We took our time, and I didn't waste a thought on the work awaiting me at home. Best of all, I didn't do it from any obligation to get the kids out into the fresh air—instead, it was an escape from the ghetto of duties which I had imposed on myself. What freedom!

Even my husband noticed the change in me. At dinner that night he said, "You look so nice in that dress—is it new?" That made my day; the dress wasn't new, but the attitude was. Perhaps my changed approach to work gave my face a new glow.

September 11
A good friend gave me some money recently. It's not for Christmas or my birthday, or for any special occasion—we aren't even short on money right now. She told me, "Do something nice for yourself. It's for you personally—don't spend it on anyone else, not even

your children. Buy something totally crazy if you're in the mood; you don't even have to tell me what you do with it. Just so you have fun."

Again, one of my attitudes about life has changed. I always used to feel guilty about allowing myself anything special, but now I'm softening that rigid attitude. In fact, I've started window-shopping and daydreaming about buying this or that with "my" money.

It's not that Hans wouldn't let me buy whatever I wanted. But I always shoved my desires aside, because other things were so much more important. I left no room for my personal wants—but now I'm learning to admit that I had plenty of desires of my own, buried deep inside of me. They don't all have to be unconditionally fulfilled, but they need to be acknowledged and appreciated, because they're part of me as a human being.

I saved the money for a long time. When I finally spent it, I valued the anticipation and the new outlook on money far more than the actual nightgown I bought myself. Because of this, Hans and I decided that each of us needs a monthly allowance to spend exactly as we wish. I'm putting "my" money into a savings account. Suddenly my long-cherished dream of learning to play the flute seems within reach. It's so much fun to look forward to something, even when it hasn't quite materialized yet! You watch a goal take shape and become clearer and nearer every day. I value this new perspective: Money is no longer an enemy to be outwitted every month; instead it's a welcome guest, anticipated eagerly.

And this new freedom has also aided my relationship with my children: When I shop for them, I do so with joy and generosity.

Chapter Three

January 5
A new year has begun; it's been a long time since I wrote in this diary. Our children fill my time completely, and I'm noticing how Hans grows into his role as father more and more. We enjoy the togetherness of parenthood, and almost every day we see some small, new progress in the children. Mark is speaking his first short sentences. Esther is walking, falling down, and pulling herself up to walk again. The experience captivates her so that she even forgets to cry.

And I am the proud possessor of a flute! It's not a German flute, but a very beautiful bass one; nevertheless I'm happy to have it. And I've found a music teacher who can give me lessons at night, when the children are in bed.

I still can't complain about a lack of work. Mark tries to do everything himself: "Me do!" And the table shows it, too, after he's fed himself. He hasn't quite caught on to the potty chair yet; I've learned not to buy delicate pants, and I've stopped ironing them!

All these beautiful experiences reawaken my old yen for having babies. Over and over the thought recurs; I can barely remember the old trials and strains. I'm going to talk to Hans about it.

February 26
Now my quiet longing has become reality. No one else knows about my precious secret yet. Just think, my third child: Your life has begun. You already exist as a tiny embryo! I barely remember coming home from the doctor's, I was so filled with excitement when I heard the result of the pregnancy test. I like knowing something that others don't even suspect. Since only you and I know that you exist, you still belong to me and to me alone. I enjoy musing about you, before anyone else gets the chance. When I get home, I'll tell your father the news. The neighbors won't find out until you get so big that I can no longer hide you. And one of these days, everyone will know—Your birth announcements will be mailed out, telling the world you're here: "The Heil family has had its third child."

But for now, you are still a tiny creature, and very close to me. I am given the privilege of carrying you around for many months. You are a You, but you are also still a part of me. I look forward to these months with you inside me: I will be your house, your food and the oxygen you breathe. I love your total dependency on me. Will there come a time, many years from now, when I am dependent upon you? It seems odd to think that I will someday be old—and you also, small unborn person, you will someday be old.

For now, I can still shelter you inside me. I look forward to these months of growth!

July 5

I always believed that pregnancy was mainly the woman's concern. I'm starting to learn just how much it requires of Hans. He too has to develop a positive response—a "yes" attitude—to my changed physical appearance. And I'm sure my fluctuating moods and worries are a trial to him.

I'm only now learning to express things which I used to keep buried deep within. I broke down and told Hans that I was afraid our child would be deformed or dead—and as soon as I started to put these vague fears into words, they completely melted away. I don't even know their source, but I see how ridiculous it is to cling to such burdens of worry. I didn't want to admit my fears because I was so ashamed of them.

What's more, my honesty gave Hans the courage to open himself up to me, too. It seems that our children continually strengthen and secure the bond of love between us. Certainly they help each of us grow in understanding of the other. What a gift children are! Having them is like possessing a well of clear cool water: Anyone who is willing to kneel down and draw from it can drink his fill.

And the bond which this gift gives our marriage helps me through the hard times of motherhood. With each additional pregnancy my sense of isolation and helplessness decreases. More and more I find a much-needed security in Hans. And how perfect, that the one who made me into a mother becomes a father through me! This intricate relationship grows through each subsequent child.

Recently Ingrid Trobisch told my husband, "The very best thing you can do for your child is to love his mother." That encouraged him, and me. I know that if our children find security, understanding, and a positive outlook on life, it will be largely due to our own happy, growing marriage. Even our unborn child can sense his father's love, because my security reflects it.

July 30
Our relatives are horrified that we're having another baby so soon after Mark and Esther. But our little family looks forward to the birth with such excitement! Often I let the children feel my tummy with their hands, especially when the baby kicks and moves noticeably. I tell them about their new little sibling-to-come. Mark comments, "Baby, wadooh, waaaah..." which means, Our baby is in there, surrounded by water. When it is born, it will already be able to cry.

And last night, after Mark had felt the new little

baby, he ran up to his father. Eagerly he pulled the shirt out of Daddy's trousers and kissed his navel—thinking a baby was hidden in Daddy's belly too. (Talk about equal rights!)

Mark is two-and-a-half years old already. He and Esther always have some new enterprise underway—and what talent they show for creating total chaos in short order! They get up earlier than anybody; this morning they climbed out of their little beds at five, and they went into the kitchen to play. It was oddly but pleasantly quiet, and I was so exhausted that I went back to sleep. When I got up, I saw the reason for the quiet: Mark was transporting oatmeal on small trucks. Esther sat on the floor between the ripped-open bags, surrounding herself with mountains of the contents and occasionally stuffing a handful into her mouth. How unspeakably exhausting and sweet those two are! I know that the dear little person inside me will be more of the same: You are wholeheartedly welcome, my child.

October 4

I am having labor pains, and I'm downright happy about it. We passed the due date a week ago, and I became so anxious to have the delivery that I mowed the whole lawn yesterday, hoping to induce labor! I stopped going shopping a while ago, because I got sick of hearing the surprised comments: "Your baby *still* hasn't come?" or, "But I thought it was due a month

Chapter Three

ago!" or even, "I bet you're going to have twins!" Well, it's finally coming.

My friend Isolde has offered to help out during the first few months after the birth. I'm infinitely thankful for that; she's already been here for a few days, and the children like her.

So I'm totally relaxed as I ride to the hospital with Hans. We chat in the car and enjoy the drive. We had this same hospital for Esther's birth. The doctor, remembering our last "team birth," promptly and totally approved our request that Hans be present. So my husband doesn't even leave my side—he's there for all the preparations, and he goes into the delivery room with me. Everything is so familiar to me now! This time I prepared with a book on natural childbirth.

Hans sits at my side like a bodyguard. I feel so secure with him here. The nurse fills out all the usual forms. Then she examines me again and runs to the telephone. I can hear her talking quickly and can't quite catch what she says—but the doctor arrives in a hurry. The contractions are getting stronger. The nurse offers me gas, to ease the pain. "You should have some," she says. "It's going to be difficult—your child is in a breech position." I don't know what to do; finally I grab the mask and press it to my face, trying to draw out all the anesthetic at once. Consequently, I'm totally dazed. There's something I want to say, but I can't get my thoughts together. There's been some kind of mistake: instead of taking the pain away, they've taken all my consciousness and my self-control! Every contraction feels like torture. I start to cry, and I search in vain for that relaxation which I practiced so often. I rack my memory, but all the techniques seem like a confused dream now. My self-control has vanished. As the last birth contraction comes, my fear peaks and at last I push with the courage of desperation.

We have a daughter. "Boy, did that go quickly for a breech birth!" says the doctor. He says only ten minutes have passed since the first contraction—but it seems like an eternity to me. Through a misty veil, I see a child lying in my arms. She is crying pitifully. Slowly it dawns on me: This is *my* child. Her head lies next to my heart. And as she quiets down, a great love awakens in me. Hans kisses me lovingly. "We have a Damaris," he says. "Aren't you happy?" Of course, I'm happy . . . but more than anything I just want to sleep and sleep and sleep.

December 10
You're a big child, my dear Damaris. You weighed nine pounds at birth, after making us wait for those seven long, fearful days. But in spite of your sturdiness, you seem so fragile to me. I think of all the difficulties you'll have to face, and I wish your parents could protect you. We can't shield you from life, but there's one thing we can, and will, do daily: We will pray that Jesus takes your life into his hands.

Chapter Three

In the meantime, for a short while, you're in my care: I even feed you completely. I think I'm a stupid mother, since I never learned to fully appropriate the joys of nursing until now! Of course, Isolde's presence is a great help; since she's still here, I can retire to the bedroom to nurse in peace. And I look forward so much to these breaks in the day when I can be available exclusively to our youngest. We have ten happy minutes together—minutes in which I'm completely free and completely relaxed and completely useful and completely happy. Lord, how wonderful it is to be a mother!

With the first child, I was so inexperienced that nursing was more trouble than joy. And the well dried up after only a few weeks. With the second child, I was always worried that the baby wouldn't be sufficiently nourished by such watery-looking stuff—although, being a nurse, I should have known better. Of course my fear had its effect on my milk supply.

So now, the third time, I've learned not to take it too seriously if the baby doesn't drink much, or wants more two hours later. I've learned such confidence that I wish it would never end; I intend to try to keep nursing as long as possible. And the whole experience vastly increases my desire for more children. I honestly believe that if more women knew the joy and satisfaction of nursing, they wouldn't be content to go without children, or to only have one or two.

February 17

Damaris, our youngest, is already four months old! She's a chubby little girl with an unusually happy and placid disposition. She hardly ever cries, and she's sleeping through the night already; she's simply no trouble at all. I attribute this largely to the fact that I'm able to continue nursing her.

The time I spend nursing is always an island of rest in the bustle of the day. I never feel guilty about being idle, because for a few precious moments I have the privilege of completing a task which is not only a job but a great gift. I'm totally secure as I provide this little person with security.

You can't understand the joy and inner peace of having a child at your breast until you've experienced it. Since I used to be very moody, I fully appreciate my new, inner serenity. How can I think of suicide, worthlessness, or incompetence when I'm being totally useful? Life looks so much brighter! This small and helpless child is fully dependent on me, and because I constantly give her whatever she needs she's growing and thriving.

But it's not so one-sided as all that; I too gain from the intimate mother-child relationship. She lies in my arms with such total trust—so helpless and yet contented with herself and her world. I see a peace in this little being which I—an adult full of experiences, expectations, and the demands of others—can no longer appropriate for myself. But this maternal happiness draws me even closer to my husband, who is such an integral part of the experience of motherhood.

I'm beginning to enjoy these weeks more and more. Without the load of worry and fear caused by my perfectionism, I can relax and have fun with Damaris. I've learned not to fuss about such trifles as unironed laundry, and so I've got more energy to do the necessary. While I occupy myself with the baby, Mark and Esther will come and sit very near me on the floor and play. I love having them all so close to me.

June 8

I'm still nursing Damaris mornings and evenings. Tonight I was sitting in the rocking chair, feeding the little one, when Esther came in and wanted to climb into my lap. I explained to her that she needed to wait until Damaris had had enough to drink. Silently she walked over to my husband, who was reading his newspaper. She shoved the large paper aside, climbed onto his lap, and unbuttoned his shirt. Then she found a comfortable position against his arm and looked for his nipple in order to suck on it. Hans and I just grinned at each other. No one said a thing. After I had put Damaris to bed, Esther came to me. "Did any milk come from Daddy?" I asked her. "It sure did," she answered gravely. She seemed to be thoroughly convinced, and thoroughly comforted.

I understand; for I'm becoming more and more aware of the pricelessness of nursing. I initially used it as a time to read, and I got acquainted with many good books that way. But now I just sit and look at my child. I admire the way she lies there and fulfills all her needs: She uses all her strength, yet she's totally relaxed—her hands make little fists, but her eyes are closed. After we've finished "working" we have fun together. I offer her a breast, and she turns away and laughs. She likes this little game, because it gives her a chance to communicate the fact that she's had enough.

June 10

Dorothy, a friend with five children, recently remarked, "One should really start having children with the third child!"

I wholeheartedly agree. My work used to control me; every day I would measure myself against how much I'd accomplished—and usually I had to give myself a bad grade. But gradually I am learning to distinguish the important from the unimportant. And new sources of strength are opening up. Every day the limits of my energy move farther out. My flute lessons continue to give me joy, and they even enable me to attack and overcome everyday tasks more efficiently. The satisfying, self-imposed job of practicing the flute gives me a new and positive approach to the work I do for my children.

Chapter Three

July 15

My periods have started again. After all these months of pregnancy it seems like an unpleasant burden to shoulder. I have to learn to accept it as an integral part of my life—a continual reminder of my womanhood. I know it's a limitation which I need to learn to live with—but I feel so irritable and unfriendly today! I'm certainly not responding sweetly to those who cross my path. Do others struggle with this problem? I remember a sentence from Ingrid Trobisch's book *The Joy of Being a Woman* (Harper & Row, 1975): "If I am living in discord with my body, I am also living in discord with my God." Today the practical application of that is for me to postpone washing the curtains until next week.

Now it's evening—and I want to record that I've survived this day after all, and it wasn't as bad as I thought it would be. When this time comes around next month, I intend to keep a firm grasp on these resolutions, and I will learn to fully accept the limitations and processes of my body.

July 17

I'm still depressed. Little daily problems are literally crushing me: the bathroom faucet leaks, the washing machine is broken, the cord has been ripped out of the iron, and I can't get the repairman to come. Piles of laundry need to be ironed and mended, the carpet needs cleaning, and the curtains are dingy with dirt. Every time I get the dishes washed, we eat off them and they're dirty again. I feel defeated by the total futility of my necessary tasks. I want to run away to some job with limits, ends, goals—a job where I can see results and have some lasting effect upon my world. I long to break out of these limited, temporal duties. I feel inferior and old-fashioned, used-up and isolated.

I still nurse Damaris at night, before I take her to bed. Often she goes to sleep in my arms. Her little face looks so satisfied when I feed her—but even nursing doesn't seem to compensate me now. I'm weary of being so tied down. And I don't feel very well physically, either. The doctor has strictly ordered me to stop nursing.

While straightening up the house, I run across a book that I've been meaning to read. It's called *Housewife by Calling,* and it's written by Elisabeth von Bibra. For some reason, I sit down in the midst of all the mess and leaf through it. One sentence strikes home: "We should not have feelings of inferiority; we need a sense of mission, because our task in this world leaves no room for feelings of inferiority."

That helps me. I consider my situation: What do I want, anyway? Aren't my children and husband the most challenging and fulfilling task I could have? Isn't developing a person the greatest and most important work I can imagine? I do believe that the rewards of caring for their well-being are worth more than the highest salary and the most ideal working conditions.

Chapter Three

September 24

The long evenings give me time to meditate on many things. I'm not nursing Damaris any more. Instead, I sit by her crib in the evenings and hold her little hand until she goes to sleep. At first she couldn't understand what had happened. She tugged at my blouse so hard that she ripped a button off, gesturing wildly in her frustration at not being able to communicate her needs. Over and over, I gently explained that she would have to do without her "sleeping medication." I could tell it was hard for her—but she was almost eleven months old.

But now I think wistfully of that intimate time of nursing. I hold Damaris in my arms a lot, and sometimes she makes herself very tiny as if she'd like to crawl back inside me again. How I wish I could give her that complete security once more!

To be honest, I'm sorry now that I didn't continue to nurse my child. I was foolish to think that I needed to set arbitrary time limits to that beautiful period. The thought has been haunting me for days. A very old evening prayer, which I learned as a child, comes back to me. I can only remember two lines clearly: "Lord, I beg that you forgive / My omission and my sin." As a child I used to wonder what "omission" was. Today I understand. But more importantly, I understand the forgiveness of my Lord for sins of omission—those sins which often we don't recognize until it's too late. How thankful I am to accept his forgiveness! I wonder how many more mistakes I'll make in raising our children. It's comforting to realize that there are no perfect parents. And I rejoice in the possibility of forgiveness.

September 30
I've just completed my evening rounds—I go from bed to bed each night, making sure that my little ones are well covered and tucked in. When I looked at our sleepers in the light of the bedside lamp, I wanted to shout for joy: what a privilege, to be the mother of these sweet kids. Children's arms to hug you—what kind of price tag could you hang on that? How wonderful to be a mother!

I believe that this indescribable enrichment in my children's presence is also the basis for a rich future. The popular goals of this twentieth century seem to be power and influence and wealth—all those empty things which break like soap bubbles in our grasp. What kind of goal does a child make? It brings responsibility. Its very presence constantly reminds us of our limitations and our mortality. I have come to determine the importance of anything by comparing it to the importance of children. For instance, concern for their future and well-being gives me the courage and energy to fight against the threats of atomic and chemical warfare. In whatever ways possible, no matter how small, I intend to work for a good future. And what reason would I have to care about following generations, if I weren't connected to them through my children?

Of course, no one can guarantee me that our children will turn out well. Every single child is a hazardous undertaking. I can only continue to invest all my love in them. But they are calculated risks, for we often find both the possibilities and the joys of accomplishment in them. And I have faith in God's power; he will enable us to fulfill our assigned tasks.

October 5
Yesterday we celebrated Damaris' first birthday. The children lovingly decorated a festive table for her, and their eyes shone as they sang "Happy Birthday." I'm impressed by the wealth of love which a child with brothers and sisters knows. Damaris was enchanted with her new hobbyhorse, and she dragged it along behind her everywhere. My youngest child, and she's already walking well and tells me when she needs to use the potty!

It's cold outside; the days are getting shorter and the nights longer. I love winter evenings when the children gather around me to tell stories or to listen to me read. The wind outside blows the last dried-up leaves off the trees and plays all kinds of games with them. The naked branches of the linden tree look like fine filigree. They let the wind shake them like dead bones. But life will reawaken in those plain gray twigs. Those hibernating buds—those buds, so inconspicuous that in winter they elude the eye of the casual observer—hold all the sleeping embryos of leaves and blooms for next spring. The warm sun will break open their jackets and lure out the fresh greens. And the flower bulbs lying under the earth will send shoots up to the light, forming buds and then beautiful blossoms. Everything awakens again, and new life unfolds all over the place!

I'm already dreaming of spring, although winter is just beginning. I'm already dreaming of another child, although the gang I have certainly creates enough work for me. It's a yearning which begins somewhere deep inside me, like the yearning for spring in nature. First life awakens in a slumbering egg; then a tiny cell starts to grow, and then it forms a person and is born. And I get to experience this firsthand, to feel the growth inside me and sense the moment of new life within. I know that this growing takes all of my strength, and I know that it will be terribly uncomfortable at times. Yet I can't help looking forward to it! I don't know when we'll have another child, but we're already ready for it. Oh, and not just one—I would bring a thousand children into the world, and raise them all, if only I were able!

Chapter Four

November 15
I've been having a lot of pain in my kidneys, and it often makes me irritable and short-tempered. Last night I could hardly sleep a wink, so I finally went to the doctor today. I'm so exhausted. The doctor tested my urine and told me I have a kidney infection. Then I asked her to run a pregnancy test. She let me watch, and I did so with great anxiety. If a change occurred on the glass dish, it would confirm a pregnancy. During the short period of waiting, something inside me cried over and over, "No, I don't want a child, not now! I'm much too weak."

The change occurred, all right: I am pregnant. I drove home very slowly. Do I really want this child, I wondered. Have I taken on too much? Perhaps our desire for more children was just a short-sighted enthusiasm. Maybe we should have given the consequences more thought. I kept thinking of the way our neighbors would react and all the curious and disapproving glances we will get. I just felt too weak, physically and emotionally, to even face them. What did I really want, anyway? Here I had longed for a child, and now that it was actually conceived it seemed like too great a load to shoulder once more. I wished I could reject it.

When I got home, Hans was waiting. I walked in the door saying, "I have a kidney infection—and we're going to have another baby." "Hallelujah!" he cried, and threw his arms around me. Didn't he even see my discouragement? I didn't feel like being hugged—I felt like giving up. I kept thinking of all the women who conceive children without wanting them and simply have abortions. I knew exactly how they felt. I felt that I had a right to shake these troubles off. And I just felt too tired to cope with the added strain of a pregnancy, piled on top of the responsibilities of my little ones. It seemed impossible; I felt as if someone had tied lead weights to me and thrown me into the depths of the sea. Dozens of negative experiences, long buried in my consciousness, rose out of the earth like giants to confront me. And my memories of the last birth planted themselves in front of me like sinister shadows.

November 21
A week has passed. Trust and desperate resistance still war within my heart—I hardly know which voice to

believe. But I'm thankful to be feeling better physically. Also, today I came across a publication by a German-Canadian mission (*The Bible For the World,* June 1972). It contained an imaginative diary of an unborn child, which touched me deeply:

5/1 Through the act of love, my parents called me into being today.

5/15 My first blood vessels are already formed, and my body's shaping up very rapidly.

5/19 I already have a tiny mouth.

5/21 Today my heart started beating on its own; who would doubt that I'm truly alive!

5/22 My mother will be so happy—I'm healthy and there's nothing for her to worry about.

5/28 My arms and legs have started growing. I can stretch out!

6/8 Little fingers are sprouting from my hands; soon I'll be able to grab with them.

6/15 My mother has finally discovered my presence—how happy I am!

6/20 Now it's obvious, to anyone, that I'm a girl!

6/24 The seeds of all my bodily organs are present in me. And I can already feel pain.

7/6 I'm starting to develop hair, and eyebrows; I'm going to look a lot better before this is through!

7/8 My eyes have been complete for a long time now, though my eyelids are still closed. I can't wait to see the whole beautiful world, and especially my dear mother who carries me.

7/19 My heart beats steadily. I feel so safe and happy!

7/20 Today my mother killed me.

I'm in the week of pregnancy where the child says, "Now it's obvious that I'm a girl! The seeds of all my bodily organs are present and I can already feel pain."

In this description, it's just somebody else's child. But the one inside me is *my* child—a little girl or boy who is unfolding inside *me*. It's growing, it can already feel pain, its small heart continually beats. Suddenly this unborn has become an Other for me, and I have a responsibility towards it, just as I have towards my children who are already born. I'm no longer thinking about a new burden; I'm thinking in terms of a new life. And my child wants to live, just as I do.

As I write this, I feel a fresh strength growing within me. Is this the positive response I've been seeking—the knowledge of a great new task? I know that the battle's not yet won; but now I have a new energy, and I can accept the fight and bring it to a good end.

December 8

Our little one is growing; I'm not going to be able to hide our secret much longer. My clothes are already too tight. I'm rather afraid to let people know about my pregnancy—now that the internal battle has been fought out, the outer warfare with our antichild surroundings will begin. So many people seem to think it's impractical, or indecent somehow, to have more than one or two children. But I love my child, and it is welcome, as far as I'm concerned. I tell it that often—I talk to it all the time. I hope that others will be able to sense my love for it.

Chapter Four

It's amazing how much God trusts me, considering how incompetent I am at times! I think I understand a little of what Mary went through—experiencing the distrust of those she trusted most, and the disapproval of all her relatives. Nevertheless, she faithfully believed God; and she told the angel, "Behold the bondslave of the Lord; be it done to me according to your word" (Luke 1:38).

Mary's example makes me capable of trusting God, even in my pregnancy.

When William came to visit us he told about his adventures in Communist-influenced countries where Christians aren't free to practice their faith. It was both refreshing and disturbing to hear him talk; the Christians in those countries are under such persecution, but they're so willing to be of service to others!

When we told him that our fourth child is on its way, he started laughing. "Would you believe what happened on my last trip?" He said, "I stayed with a couple and their eight children. The apartment was very small, and the guestroom was obviously the place where they slaughtered the pigs. Equipment for butchering was evident in my room, and a big hook hung right over my bed! In spite of the close quarters, I felt a wonderful peace in this family. They weren't quiet, by any means, but the atmosphere was especially loving. Naturally, we got to talking about children. When my host and hostess heard that my wife and I have only two children, they fell silent in dismay. Finally the father of the family said, 'Brother, we will pray that the Lord gives you more!'"

What faith these people have—in spite of their situation, they seem to view children as a very special gift of God.

December 14

My kidney infection has healed, and I find my strength returning. My response to this new child is, slowly but surely, growing into a true pleasure of anticipation. In fact, I notice that this pregnancy seems to encumber me much less than the previous ones did. I'm even more emotionally stable. And Hans, too, is changing and growing: he's far more responsive to my feelings than he was in earlier pregnancies—in fact, I'm starting to feel that he really understands me!

I noticed that especially today, when I told him of a new fear. Rubella—"German measles"—is currently going around. It's a normal childhood ailment, which usually runs its course quite harmlessly. But if a pregnant woman contracts in the first three months of pregnancy, her unborn child can be seriously damaged. I never had rubella as a child, and now I fret that I will catch it and our little one will be harmed.

But Hans prays with me about such fears, and I'm greatly comforted. Like a mountain climber scaling the highest peaks, he continually puts my problems in his backpack and carries them up to the throne of our Father in Heaven. What a great gift my husband is!

Chapter Four

April 8

A few days ago Hans came home with a box of chocolates for me—in spite of the fat of my sixth month! He happily watched me gobble them down, and I could find no trace of reproach in his face. That made me feel so rich, because he's truly learned to accept me and love me the way I am.

It wasn't always that way: during the first two pregnancies he kept a lion's watch over my weight, rationing out compliments so carefully that he only succeeded in discouraging me deeply. I felt even less inclined to eat moderately, because I felt so unappreciated and misunderstood. So I comforted myself with sweets, and the pounds kept piling on. And anger built up inside of me, towards the child whom I blamed for making me fat.

All this makes me doubly thankful for my husband's increased devotion; I'm so glad that he gives me small compliments instead of swats on the hand! True, he doesn't bring me dozens of red roses—but all I need is a single flower from time to time. And sometimes the headiness of our early being-in-love days rises within me again.

We're preparing for the birth together. Ingrid Mitchell's book *Giving Birth Together: The Modern Parents' Home Program of Natural Childbirth Exercises* (Continuum Publishing Co., 1975) has been a great help. Not only does she give excellent advice for relaxation and muscle-building exercises, but she shows how the husband can prepare both his wife and himself for the birth.

So Hans takes an intense interest in my changing experiences now! He lays his ear on my abdomen to listen to his child's heartbeat, and then he draws crosses on my belly with a ball-point pen—he's always so proud to have found the right place! But I understand his joy; it's the joy of no longer being left out, of becoming an active participant in my creative process. He finds satisfaction in these activities, and they make me happy too. I see them as a basis for my own personal liberation from fear and feelings of being misunderstood. These hours together free us from the memories of past problems. They lead us into new depths of openness to experience.

June 23

About four weeks ago I experienced some light bleeding. I had to lie still in the hospital for eight days—they wouldn't even let me get out of bed. Then I went home with nothing to show for it, after promising to return to the hospital at the very first sign of labor, or on my due date, whichever came first. And tomorrow is the day: a Sunday. Since we've already packed the children off to my mother's, it's very peaceful here at home. They love to stay with her anyway, so it doesn't bother me to be separated from them for such a short time. The two girls, especially, can't wait to see the baby I've hidden in my belly for so long. They made me promise to be sure to bring it home with me!

My own thoughts constantly revolve around that small person inside me—that new person whom I will see soon. At first it could move in its quarters with great freedom; but by now they must be terribly cramped—they must enclose it like a jail. It moves vigorously, like it's searching for an exit—a doorway to a new world of space and freedom. I lay my hands on my abdomen and talk to my child. "Soon, very soon," I comfort it, "you'll be able to kick as freely as you wish!"

And once more Hans will be with me all through the birth. Since he's already "gone through labor" three times, his presence doesn't seem to bother the doctors anymore.

June 24

This morning the medical superintendent came into my room to examine me. I hardly know him; he's never taken care of me during delivery before. He went over everything once more, and noted it all down. Then he remarked, "You have three children already, don't you?"

"Yes," answered, "and I'm very happy with them."

"Then this will be your fourth child. At birth, when the child's head is passing through, we usually give women an anesthetic. If you give your consent, we'll sterilize you right after the birth. It's only minor surgery. Then when you wake up you'll have gotten it all over with."

Shock held me speechless for a moment. I'm not easily upset, but this made me furious. "Gotten it over with? I'm looking forward to this birth—I'm looking forward to holding my child in my arms right after it's born. I've waited nine months to touch this little one, and now I'm supposed to sleep through its coming, anesthetized? And why should I be sterilized? Is having children such a terrible calamity? Are four children more than anyone could possibly handle?"

I started to dissolve into tears. I tried to hold them back, because I was girding myself to fight a whole battle for the sake of my child. I love the child within me, and I love my children who have already been born—but I also love all those who are yet to be given me. If I were sterilized, I would feel like a well without water; like a person who chooses to be crippled, out of laziness; like a house which I lock and board up so it can't offer anyone else a place of safety. It would be like sawing off the limb that connects me to the tree of life, or absent-mindedly tossing a key to buried treasure into the fire. All these thoughts flared up and burst in my head like fireworks.

The doctor left the room rather quickly. He mumbled some kind of excuse as he closed the door behind him.

Now that I've cooled down, I'm still upset. Am I the only one who feels this way? The doctor certainly spoke as if he represented the interests of many. Perhaps I'm abnormal—but I know I couldn't bear the finality of sterilization. It would rob me of an important option—an opportunity which enriches my life even when I don't take advantage of it.

My distress is turning into prayer. I will ask God for a good delivery. When Hans comes into the room, I can tell he senses my oppression. I can't bring myself to talk about it, so I just lean my head against his shoulder and feel his arms close about me. We are silent. Slowly a sense of security returns to me; I feel as if this embrace encloses our whole family. Hans is a safe nest in which I can lay my child. And God seems close enough to reach out and touch. Actually, I know that he's even nearer to me than that: after all, he himself created this new life within me. And our desire to pass on life is given and approved by God.

June 25
This morning I had strong labor pains. Hans stayed with me all day. I asked him to get me a magazine with lots of pictures to look at, to help take my mind off the pain. So what did he bring me? "Festive Meals for All Occasions"—oh, these men! He never stopped to think that I've had almost nothing to eat for two days now. It was mouth-watering: I viewed photos of juicy, brown roasts, cool ice cream in the heavy summer heat, and delightful icy drinks. It certainly did divert me!

Then my labor began in earnest, so we started our "collective examination." Here was our big chance to try out what we had practiced for so long, and we were frankly excited about the opportunity to "perform" well. Hans tested my relaxation, timed the intervals between contractions, and reminded me of the correct way to breathe. The doctor rarely even stuck his head into the delivery room, because my cervix wasn't dilated very far. But, because of my relaxation, I could feel it opening wider and wider. I was sharply aware of every phase of the birth, and I knew it couldn't last much longer. When the doctor came in to examine me, I felt sick and asked him to take my blood pressure. The nurse arrived with the apparatus—just in time to catch the head of our daughter! The perineum hadn't even ripped. The doctor, who was closing the door behind him, stormed over and finished the birth.

I overheard him remark to the nurse, "These are the kind of people who suddenly have their children in the elevator, on the way up here." But he was wrong, for my labor pains *were* severe. It had taken all my concentration to relax and breathe correctly—and the doctor seemed merely irritated that I'd lain there so calmly, without moaning.

I had a strong impulse to immediately let my little one drink at my breast. She was crying so miserably that I wanted to comfort her. But when I asked if I could nurse her, the request was turned down with a superior smile. Finally, after everybody left, I held my child close to me. She closed her mouth firmly around my nipple and suckled. The crying stopped, and my little one became calm. The connection between mother and child, which had been so traumatically severed, seemed to form again.

Hans and I looked at our child with joy—and then we turned to look at each other. "You were simply wonderful," he whispered.

I could only answer, "Darling, so were you. This time, we have truly given birth together."

I am irresistibly reminded of our wedding vows: "Will you ... love, honor, and cherish ... in joy and sorrow, in sickness and health, till death do you part?" It seems to me that the "I do" resounds in my ears like a mighty clap of thunder and unites with the powerful strains of an organ hymn: "Holy, holy, holy, Lord God Almighty..." Everything in me sings along like a roaring ocean of praise. I feel as if I've dissolved into a million strings, and each is competing with the others in exultation. And it all harmonizes perfectly, in myself, in my husband, in my child....

After every birth, it was the baby's first cry that brought me out of pain and into joy: *My child is here, and it's alive! I've endured all the discomfort, and now I have my reward.* But this time another idea occurred to me. I saw my little girl's face grimacing in pain, and I realized that she had just lived through a horrible experience. Her cry was a desperate call for help. The little one was squeezed, pressed, and shoved all over during the labor. And afterwards it hurt me to see her grabbed by the legs, measured, and put into tight clothing like a doll, before she was even brought to her mother. I wanted to shelter her in my arms, to hold her close and comfort her after all she'd gone through.

June 28
Miriam—so here you are! A small, dear human child has arrived on this vast earth. I hold you in my arms and feel you lying so very close to me, and I still can't fathom that you were previously that kicking entity in my abdomen. You lie there, completely trusting yet completely helpless. Just think, I am privileged to feed you, to teach you to walk, to raise you to adulthood . . . and to embrace you and to let you embrace me. Am I not to be envied? We love you, our child.

I remember the night after you were born. I lay in my bed, listening to the crying from the nursery, and wondering if you, our Miriam, were one of those awake and unhappy infants. I wanted to go and comfort you; but a sterile door stood solidly between us. They would never allow me to go in there and pick you up. My poor child, they made you come out of my warm enclosure, and then they took you away from me, and they wouldn't even let you stay and snuggle up. This hospital situation makes me doubly eager to go home!

The birth is still an exciting, moving memory. The endless beauty of passing through those hours with Hans—the wonder of it culminated in the first cry of our child. How can you describe moments like that? They are high points of our life, times when we see a bit of God's creative power deep within ourselves, and we understand his love afresh. And we experienced it together! What impetus and meaning this gives to our marriage—in our child we see the reality of what we longed for so often in our deepest hours of reflection, in the beating of our hearts, in our most intimate moments together: In the child we are one body, one heart, one soul.

June 30
A prayer: My God, how great you are. You enrich every mother in the world when you entrust to her a bit of your creative power. How amazing that you let me understand a part of your greatness; sometimes I feel myself losing all ties to this earth, I'm so full of wonder at your eternal love. Like a swift bird, I soar up into infinity. But I'm also a chick under the wings of a hen: I feel secure because I can provide this security for others.

Lord, thank you that I am a woman. Thank you that I am Hans' wife. And thank you that I am a mother. Lord, I'm so grateful for each valuable little piece of creation that you've entrusted to me. How bountifully you bless us!

July 10
I'm happy to be home from the hospital. Whenever I look back on this pregnancy, I'm grateful all over again for the ways in which it drew Hans and me closer together. But I also remember my fear of contracting

rubella. I asked the doctor to inoculate me, in case I get pregnant again. So when I left the hospital, he said, almost mockingly, "Good-bye, till next time!" But I certainly hope we won't meet again. Next time, I believe I would choose another doctor.

The children are beside themselves with joy. They want to have Miriam on their laps all day long. Everything amazes them: the little fingers, the small head, the sparse growth of hair. They're all too eager to find out whether their little sister can walk yet. She gets a hundred kisses every day. It's delightful to watch them accept the little newcomer into their midst.

Anne, a nursing student, has come to help us out for eight weeks. We get along beautifully. Over and over I'm impressed by how God sends help at crucial times of need. This will give me time to regain my strength.

September 6

Miriam lies in my arms, drinking. These moments of nursing are always oases of peace for me. They lose nothing of their beauty, intimacy, and power, in spite of their frequency. When I look back on the last few years of my life, I can see a point where my relationship to my children changed decisively: The time of my great discovery was a mountain peak which widened my little world and my tiny horizon to dizzying expanses. An undreamed-of treasure chest opened up; roads appeared and pointed to goals which I hadn't known existed.

But all this didn't occur loudly or violently, and I doubt that it was visible to others. The light slowly dawned within me, turning my whole self around. My very world took on fresh color, and I began to breathe easily. This turning point was the time when I discovered that nursing isn't just a necessity for the baby; the mother also needs this procedure, to teach her about her relationship with the child. After I had overcome my sense of helplessness, nursing helped me to understand the beauty of life—my life, our life.

June 10
A long time has passed since I wrote in here. Our children bring as much joy, but they have all the usual little childhood ailments. I really get worn-out from lack of sleep whenever they're sick. We emptied our bedroom and made it into a nursery, so the children have more room. We didn't use our bedroom all day long, anyway. Now we sleep on a pullout couch in the living room, and this new arrangement seems to work out well.

But last night was terrible: Mark had a painful muscle cramp, Esther couldn't breathe and kept asking for nose drops, and Damaris kept coming and climbing in bed with me. I finally carried her back to her own bed, after she had fallen soundly asleep. But then Miriam fell out of her crib and began to sob. What an accumulation of disturbances, for one night! It again makes me aware of the fact that having children means anything *but* comfort, independence, and pure unalloyed happiness. In fact, it makes me long to pack my bags tomorrow and leave. I want to shrug off all my responsibilities and once more find myself free and unattached.

But when am I truly free? Does freedom really mean independence? I imagine what my life would be like with no children or husband:

"I live in a beautiful apartment at the edge of the city. The alarm wakes me in the morning; I've slept wonderfully all night long. After getting up and taking a shower, I enjoy a peaceful breakfast, with lovely music in the background. No one interrupts me—no one asks about homework, pants, shirt, or sandwiches. But no one kisses me either; no one shares his thoughts with me, or asks for my opinion. On the bus I recognize a few faces, but I don't know any names. Everything's so impersonal. At the office I find distant friendliness, work, irritating pressures. In the evening I return to my apartment. No one greets me, or asks how my day went. I have peace, and I'm alone."

Is that what I really want? Who, among my acquaintances, would I change places with? The turmoil inside me subsides. No, I wouldn't trade lives with anyone in the whole world! Having children does mean hard, and almost continual, work. Over and over I'm forced to admit my own failure and my dependence upon God. But underneath it all, I don't really want complete independence. Freedom sounds so desirable—

but who can live totally free of every law, or wholly independent of other people? I couldn't do it. That very self-assumed freedom would cause such conflicts within that I would be unhappy, despairing, and quite unfree at the deepest level. I believe that only by living in obedience to Jesus' will for our lives can we be truly free.

July 28
Earlier this summer, the doctor advised us strongly to take the children to the mountains for the sake of their health. So now we have wonderful memories of our vacation in Austria with our four little acrobats. The fact that I'm still nursing thirteen-month-old Miriam made the whole thing possible; it ensured that I always had a "bottle" handy, with milk neither sour nor too cold nor too hot. Good thing that nursing isn't a hassle for me anymore—it's finally become a very natural part of our lives. In fact, everyone takes it for granted but me; and I still find it a great source of private joy.

How wonderful to share new sights and experiences as a family! One lovely summer day we all took a boat ride on the lake. One drizzly, rainy day we hiked up into the mountains: we had a snowball fight on one peak, we admired both the huge scenic views and the tiny, splendidly-colored flowers, and we shivered through a thunderstorm in a cable car hanging over the valley. We sang at the top of our lungs as we watched the lovely lakes glide by. We treated ourselves to ice cream ... sometimes we all slept together in the large bed, getting up early to catch the sunrise, or sleeping in late as we pleased. One night we didn't wash before going to sleep because we were afraid of a large moth which had occupied the bathroom. We read old Bible stories aloud, and they seemed new and fresh because our hearts were opened up by new experiences. Both Hans and I learned a more simple and direct relationship with God; I felt that I had actually "become as a little child" again during those days. How could we have done any of this without our children?

December 14
Miriam is almost eighteen months old—what a long time I've been able to nurse her! What a very special, beautiful, and rich time, too: we could never have been separated from each other for more than a few hours at a time. Our periods of nursing were always a return to close communion. And I never felt tied down during this time; it didn't seem like a prison, even though it ruled out a lot of things I would have liked to have done. Those happy moments, which added such richness to my life, far outweighed anything I gave up for their sake.

In fact, the nursing encouraged me in the midst of all my work. I felt like a flower, finally unfolding to my full glory, and accepting both the rays of the sun and the chill of the rain as necessities in my daily life. I survived the night's chill because my life was deeply rooted in God. Even wild thunderstorms rarely disturbed my spirits!

But this time is finally over. Miriam lies sleeping in my arms; she wouldn't even drink at my breast tonight, though I offered it several times. Every child acts as a building block for the next. So with Miriam I succeeded in correcting the mistake I'd made with Damaris: I realize now that it's best to let the child determine the time for weaning.

December 18
When I was a little girl, I remember being on a bus where a middle-aged woman and her grandchild sat across from me. The little child poured out a continual stream of questions, about anything and everything he saw through the window. The grandmother got more and more impatient, and finally she snapped, "Just for a change, why don't you try leaving me in peace for five minutes?"

At the time, I was indignant about such an unloving attitude: I would have delighted in answering the child. I was irritated that she didn't appreciate having such a bright and curious grandchild.

Nowadays, I understand the woman's feelings only too well! I hear the word "why" from morning till night: "Why do some trees have leaves, but others have needles?" "Why does a rainbow have so many colors?" Or, "Will I get my own bed in Heaven? Can I take my doll when I go to Heaven?" and, "Mommy, when the Lord Jesus comes back someday, you'll remember to take our house key, won't you?" Sometimes I field questions until I'm exhausted. And sometimes I'm impatient, just like the woman on the bus—whatever happened to my gift of listening to others? I guess you need to stand in someone else's shoes before judging them!

I'd rather stay immersed in my own thoughts and ignore all the little voices pleading for attention. But how can my children get to know the world, how will they ever understand relationships, if I don't answer their questions? Often I just listen silently; and secretly, inside, I'm hoping they will shut up soon. I want to learn to take the children's questions as seriously as I'd like mine to be taken. I especially need to learn to make my ears sensitive to their fears; it takes deep "listening between the lines" to understand what makes them upset. There's constant tension between my time schedule and many chores, and my children's conception of time. Over and over I have to push aside other things in my life to make a space for my children. It's important to do this without losing myself in the process. I do want to learn to set aside a half-finished task without dissatisfaction because it's not completed.

I used to wonder why the angels went to the shepherds in the field to announce the good news of Jesus' birth. It must have been because the shepherds dared to risk loss by leaving their sheep behind. They hurried to the stable, knowing that even the greatest loss meant nothing in light of that wonderful happening. And so they were privileged to find the child.

January 25
Today I'm twenty-eight years old. I received plenty of beautiful gifts—but the ones I love best are our children.

I just looked in on the four little sleepers. After filling the house with noise less than an hour ago, they've all gone off and all you can hear is the sound of regular breathing. I switched on the night light, and looked at each child lovingly. How different they are! Each has the same parents, but each has a personality all his own. And they each mean something very special to me. Long ago, I remember hearing that a child from a large family had died, and I thought how much less sad that was than if a couple had lost their only child. Now I know how wrong I was. Every child is a unique personality, and completely irreplaceable. So I love each child as if he were my only one.

Empress Maria Theresa, mother of sixteen children, once said that a mother's love is not divided but multiplied. I understand how she felt. My love isn't proportioned out to each of our four rascals—instead, each child owns me completely as his or her mother. I think every person needs to know that he's a unique individual. In the same way, God doesn't love me as part of an immense mass of humanity, but as one person, myself. Jesus died for me as if I were the only one who needed him to, as though he loved only me. I'm just beginning to comprehend that. Again, I'm learning a wonderful truth through my children.

March 8

In a calendar called "Woman and Mother," I've found a saying by François Lombardi: "Only a fool would maintain that he sees no sense in what a child tells him."

That's so true with me and our children! Each one acts as a mirror to show me who I really am. I'm coming to know my own limitations and my bad reactions—but I also continually discover new gifts and abilities. And along with each new child a fresh bit of patience, a greater measure of strength, and an increase of love is born in me. As often as I'm made aware of my limits I'm brought back to dependence upon God. His power is inexhaustible, and he can give even when my own strength runs out.

And my reactions reveal my capacities. Often I fail and find myself doing the very opposite of what I desire. But at least that keeps me from arrogance, and it gives me incentive to work on myself. Of course no one's handing me patience on a silver platter; but I've been given the prerequisites to the learning of patience! So all failure has its positive side: the chance to learn and thus succeed the next time. Each of my children is an opportunity for experience—and I think that growth and self-improvement are more valuable than jewels.

Chapter Four

May 5
Dying and being born run their course in nature. We see that as a natural cycle, a necessity for the renewal of life. The fresh, bright green of the young beech trees, the small yellow dandelion suns in the overgrown grass, the warm sun and the cool wind, and the constant music of the birds—these things give us inklings of the joy of taking part in creation. When the dawn breaks, dew fills the grass and the air comes alive with chirping and singing. Man and animal alike express their wonder at the miracle of life. Living in this harmony, this luminosity, this warmth, is like holding a piece of eternity. I often remember something from the Old Testament: "We were like those who dream. Then our mouth was filled with laughter, and our tongue with joyful shouting" (Psalm 126:1b-2).

August 15
On Sunday I went into the children's room to announce dinner. But I remained silent by the door, struck by the harmony of the scene within. There they stood, my three lively little ladies and my rascal, and all four pairs of children's eyes riveted to their father's hands. Hans was trying to glue together the supports of their broken blackboad. Their hope that all would be well again, their certainty that Dad would succeed, their pride in him and their happiness at being taken seriously—all these emotions were obvious, and they touched me deeply.

I rarely see my husband as relaxed and engrossed as he is in the hours he spends with the children. I love to stand at the door and listen quietly; I think I get to know him better in such moments, and I grow to love him more.

October 29
We've had a most trying weekend. A married couple with many questions and problems came to stay with us, hoping to find some help through counseling. In spite of my exhaustion, I rejoice to think of some of the answers and solutions which we discovered together, through conversation.

We've never been in such demand for pastoral care and advice as we are now! At the very moment when God began to give us children, our ability to counsel others seemed to improve. And I notice that each additional child awakens new gifts within us; we've especially grown in our ability to sympathize with others' peculiar situations. Often we're questioned about problems for which we have no solutions. But even after such encounters we receive thankful letters. Why? I think that perhaps we're able to pass on a bit of our own sense of security in God. Security must be a rare commodity in these troubled times. Our children are the ones who have made us so capable of showing love, of allowing our security to become visible to others—because they themselves live out their direct, childlike natures in front of us day by day.

Chapter Four

February 2

My self-confidence grows with every child. Our culture is so critical of any family larger than one or two children that it used to make me fearfully self-conscious to take our three children shopping. But no longer; today I walked proudly through the city with our four little ones. And I felt self-conscious, this time, because of my great wealth. After all, we see a millionaire in quite a different light from an ordinary laborer; and how much more precious my children are than millions!

I wonder if my changed attitude is noticeable to others. Just today, I had two positive experiences: First an elegantly dressed lady stopped me on the street, and said politely, "Please excuse me, but are those your children?" Yes, I said, they are. And she answered, "Oh, you seem so happy with them! Now I regret that I had only two children. I just didn't want to spoil my comfortable life; and now it's too late. But I'm very happy for you."

And then in the parking lot a Mercedes stopped as we were getting into our car. The driver got out, pointed to our children, and said with a kind smile, "I have four of those—marvelous, isn't it?"

Oh, what rich investments these children are! Every human being is an investment in the future and can bring great profit. And I'm very thankful for my own personal "investments"; they have changed my life so much, and always for the better. Ingrid Trobisch has meant a lot to me in my experience of motherhood. I wrote her this letter for her birthday:

"A hug of thankfulness to you on this anniversary of your coming into being! I'm glad that your parents got married, and that they received you as a gift instead of choosing to remain childless out of selfishness. If it hadn't been for them, mankind would have been the poorer by a 'luxury item' which even the rich can't buy—that priceless gift that everyone longs for: a person whose love and understanding reach many helpless, stranded people with new hope, whose sympathy causes even arrogant people to reflect. Sometimes your unusual gifts stir up foolish people to ridicule—but continue on your way bravely. We—and I speak for all those to whom you have become a signpost—we thank God for you."

Chapter Five

March 16
Mark is seven years old now! He and Esther both go to school, and they love it. Damaris, at four, attends kindergarten. She can't wait until Miriam's third birthday, when our youngest will be able to accompany her.

And now—our fifth child is on the way! We're all excited about it. The birth is still five months away, but Mark and the girls can hardly wait. The children put their hands on me to feel the baby's movements, and they want to know *right now* whether it's a boy or a girl. The desires for a brother or a sister are equally divided. But they're completely united in the pursuits of collecting toys for the new baby and thinking of names they like. This time of preparation is made truly beautiful by the fact that so many people share in my joy every day. We have already claimed the little unborn as ours.

Ingrid Trobisch impressed me with her account of

her mother's attitude: when she had given birth to five children, she prayed for five more! Suddenly, I understand this woman, and I admire her; she trusted God enough to look beyond her own horizons, because she understood the principle of investing in the future. I don't yet have the courage to look forward to the next child so soon. To me, each new child is a step into the unknown, a journey to a strange land. But Hans and I are prepared to go a step further, whenever the time is right. We're willing to remain open and flexible; we don't want to lay the question of another child aside like a finished chapter. We don't worry about the inconvenience of it, for we gain so much in return for our lost comfort. We want and need children for their sakes, and also for our own.

Gottfried Keller says: "Man indifferently passes many a paradise garden, only to mourn when he returns and finds the gates locked."

Our opportunity to have children is one of those paradise gardens. Many pass it by indifferently—and they never miss it until the door is closed.

May 15

It's a little past 4 A.M. My little ones sleep peacefully, dreaming on into the new day. Even their mouths are still, for once! I am sitting at the window; a light mist lies over the forests—an indescribably beautiful scene.

How amazing, the ways our lives change again and again. I think I don't have the same physical strength, in this pregnancy, as I used to. Many chores simply don't get done. I tire more easily, get nervous more often, and find myself more inwardly focused than before.

I've learned to live by cues from my body, and I'm more aware of its need for rest. I just can't totally exhaust myself all the time. Days which are very draining, because of conversations and visitors, need to be followed by relaxing lulls. Obviously, I learn something new in every pregnancy! I didn't take care of myself at all until the third child, and only starting with the fourth pregnancy did I find time for all the activities and hobbies which now bring me such joy.

But even though I get so tired now, there are new compensations. I'm finding great depth in things which used to barely move me. I never cease to wonder at the way that the growth of each new life transforms me, renews me, changes me. Sitting here and writing on into the new day like this is a novel experience; usually, at this stage of pregnancy, I'm still in bed this time of day—worn-out and foolishly wishing for more sleep.

So each of these special times in my life—each pregnancy—initiates me further into the beauties of life. I'm learning to master life, and to enjoy it more fully. In fact, with each pregnancy I receive more strength—not so much physical strength as an inner energy which leads to great bursts of creativity. I feel a strong incentive to work towards something significant and purposeful. Of course I don't always rise above my circumstances, but I'm more capable of controlling certain situations. Today the chaos in our home particularly depressed me, and it paralyzed all my efforts to start the morning's tasks. So I sat down on a chair in the middle of the kitchen, and painted a clothes hanger. Then I was able to get up and cheerfully start on my work.

June 18
The adjacent apartment in our house was vacant, so the landlord gave us permission to break through the wall. Now we have three more rooms: we're in a real bedroom again, Mark is enjoying his own little realm, and the girls are excited about all the possibilities. But because of the increase in rent we have to economize in other things. My passion for beautiful old furniture must remain unsatisfied for a while. Nevertheless, we have all the wonderful open country outside, with living forests visible through our windows like oil paintings; and what's more, we have a happy family here inside.

There are even a few people here in our little village who rejoice with us in the coming of this new child. I treasure my encounters with these individuals! Mrs. Lambert, a middle-aged woman, has five children, and she loves each one as if it were the first and only. She shared her diary with me, and with her permission I will pass on an excerpt:

"Two boys followed the births of our two girls. So

we had two little pairs, which in spite of all the work was a beautiful experience. All those people who called us 'behind the times' and 'old-fashioned' would have been envious if they had known of our quiet happiness. When our fifth baby began to grow within me, the large eyes of our older children began to survey me wonderingly. They watched me silently, hanging on me like question marks, until one day Freddie finally asked, 'Mother, where do babies come from?'"

I love the matter-of-fact joy with which our children are accepting the idea of another sibling. Esther, seven years old, is lying next to me on the floor and building a zoo. Just now she remarked, "You hope the baby's a boy, don't you?" "Yes," I answered, "but not because boys are better—it's just that we already have three girls." "And after that," she responded promptly, "we'll want another brother so we can be even!"

Mrs. Roth, one of the people I mentioned above, tells me, "I can't wait for your baby to come—I'll have to drop by often and see it. I envy you for the little person growing inside you; you'll have the joy of seeing him grow up, of directing his helpless hands and teaching his mouth to speak."

And another encouraging person is Mrs. Bastian, a retired midwife. She still sees children as a miracle from God. She's not old-fashioned, she just understands something of the connection between a child and joy, between a child and fulfillment, between a child and wealth. We're glad that she appreciates the blessing of our children.

Isn't this what we really want, as women—the privilege of being a mother? I believe that this desire is present in every woman; but many bury it under the debris of prejudice, negative experiences, false expectations, and foolish talk. In fact, hopes and dreams of self-fulfillment are deep-seated in every human being—but for women the answer is so close and available.

The few positive voices are countered by many negative ones. The one that hurt me most was the derogatory remark of a ten-year-old: "I bet she wants to populate the world by herself and make sure that we won't die out." I'm sure he didn't know what he was saying, and was only echoing his parents' ideas. But I think his statement implied a judgment on himself: "I am unneeded, unwanted."

Happily, such unwanted children often become the sunshine of the whole family. I've met many women who are deeply grateful that an abortion failed and the child was born anyway, and others who joyfully tell how an unwanted child became a special blessing. One woman who made a deep impression on me told me that she had constantly abused her husband after the conception of an unwanted child, and it took her years to forgive him. "I am deeply ashamed of that," she said, "and I had to pray and beg God for forgiveness. In fact, that very child brought us unusual joy, and even though he's grown up now we're still particularly close."

Jesus was one of those unplanned children, and he

was unwanted by almost everyone. Walter Trobisch's book *Love Yourself: Self Acceptance and Depression* (InterVarsity Press, 1976) portrays this clearly: Jesus was a disgrace to his relatives, a mystery to the man who had to take on the role of father, a trial of faith for a chaste woman. But it was Jesus who brought us redemption; an unwanted child was the salvation of the world!

And we are wanted, even when we are unwanted. God wants us. He created us in his image, to have loving fellowship with him. His love overcomes the broken pieces of our weak abilities. He's willing to make us into useful vessels from which others can draw strength.

July 15
It's oppressively hot. We can hardly stand to be in our apartment, and the heat bothers me especially because of my pregnancy. So we decided to all get out and go swimming together. As we got out of the car at the pool, we were hit by sympathetic glances, open disapproval, and laughter. Other people's derision still gets to me—I felt like sticking my tongue out at them! Good thing Hans was with us.

So now I sit and mull over the response these people make to our family. Is it because of their own disillusionment with life, the fact that their parents didn't accept them, or a desire for total freedom? They only know a caricature of that would-be freedom; I think they've robbed themselves of it through their own stupidity, backwardness, or indifference. I'm starting to feel a deep sympathy for these people who used to make me so mad. They don't really know life or freedom; they've never experienced either responsibility or joy. They're satisfied to barely skim the surface of life and never know true fulfillment.

Why is our age so heartless and arrogant? I believe it's the attitude of many toward children; they're treated as negligible or irrelevant to existence. At best they're tolerated as troublesome peripheral figures. But children are the ones who characterize a people, and we've become a people deficient in children. This deficiency marks all areas of life, but more than anything it's affected one-on-one relationships, which are often crass and indifferent these days. The ties between many people are like rootless trees—they're stranded in immobility like ships in shallow water. They see marriage and the family as prisons which will lock them in and rob them of their freedom; they don't realize that within those "walls" the very roots of freedom find their proper soil.

Children do require time, strength, money, and solid nerves; and we tend to think we have no time or strength to spare from this fast-paced life. Our modern nerves are too weak to put up with a little screamer, an impatient question-asker, and an endless noisemaker. Often children tire us during the day and keep us up late at night. Are they really a gift, in spite of all this?

Chapter Five

I remember the first period of my walk with Jesus. Before I gave him my yes, I was afraid to let go of my old life—I dreaded becoming like this or that "fossilized" Christian. But I decided completely for Christ and gave him all of myself—and then I found such undreamed-of joy, and dozens of new doors suddenly opened to me! I had feared renunciation, and through it I found life and complete satisfaction. Something similar is happening in my experience with our children; the more I prepare to believe God rather than my own "rational" arguments, the more strength and satisfaction I find. Whoever lives in obedience to God's word will receive the power that stands behind it.

July 29
You're moving inside me today, wholly you and yet completely me too: My dear little human! I lie very still, full of wonder at your declaration of independent life. When I feel your little hands and feet moving, I'm boundlessly happy that I can shield you so completely in the soft, warm hollow of my body. It's good to be able to protect you for a few more months, far from the strife and insecurity of this world, and far from its problems and pains.

You're still now; have you fallen asleep, or are you just daydreaming? The rhythm of my heart beats in your ears—day and night, night and day. It's a part of your world; it belongs to you. One of these days it will be stilled, and you'll be shoved into a new, confusing world. But even then I'll give you a home and protect you: I'll hold you very close and press your little ear against my heart. Then you'll know that I'm still here, that I still love you, that my heart still beats for you. We belong together. And when you someday fly out on your own, my little bird, the nest you leave behind will always be kept warm for you.

August 8
In spite of all my good memories of past births, I've been extremely moody lately. Today is a down day. We're expecting our little one in five weeks. But I feel so unfit for a birth; sometimes fear latches on to me — fear of failure, and fear of death. ("Will our child be healthy?" "Who would take care of our four lively children, if I never returned home from the hospital?") I hate my thoughts, and I try to drive them away, but I can't. All these negative mental images haunt me and destroy my joy in my work. Some days I get very little done, because the fears paralyze my limbs like a malicious illness. I scold myself for allowing these images to imprison me.

   Yet — behind my worries likes the shadow of reality. How close together life and death have moved in my consciousness! Every day we should be prepared for either. After all, we were made for eternity. And I know my life is worth living because it's intended for eternity. My child reminds me of that, and keeps me from living on a superficial level. True, this process often takes my breath away and fills my heart with fear. But I'm also traveling deeper into the depths of being and its beauties; again, joy and renunciation are inextricably connected. Joy has its price: I have to give up a self-centered life. My child wants to be born, and so it tears itself loose from me. And we both will have to find ourselves anew. All of that is painful. But the process of separation is necessary, if we're ever to see each other face to face. How precious! I'm returning from the depths, and I notice that I'm richer than when I went down.

Besides, my "devotional password" for today is 1 Peter 5:7—"Casting all your anxiety upon him, because he cares for you." That speaks to me, and to all of us. God cares! Slowly jubilation breaks through me: I'm not alone in the depths, anymore than I'm alone on the high places. He cares, and he carries, and he takes us through.

August 10
My whole attitude toward birth has been altered by a book. In Frederick Leboyer's *Birth Without Violence* (Alfred A. Knopf, 1975), I found my unexpressed feelings put into words—in fact, it spells out my sentiments exactly. I've always had the instinctive desire to give birth to my child in familiar surroundings, far away from glinting instruments, loud noises, and strangers. And I've always wanted to have the baby very close to me right after birth, to touch it gently and show

it my love. But now I've realized that the experience of birth is horrible for the child. Dr. Leboyer describes what he sees when he looks closely at a newborn:

> The child?
> Oh, dear God, it can't be true!
> This mask of agony, of horror. These hands—above all, these hands—clasping the head...
> This is the gesture of someone struck by lightning. The gesture you see in the mortally wounded, the moment before they die.
> Can birth hold so much suffering, so much pain? While the parents look on in ecstasy, oblivious....
> What makes being born so frightful is the intensity, the boundless scope and variety of the experience, its suffocating richness.
> People say—and believe—that a newborn baby feels nothing. He feels everything.
> Everything—utterly, without choice or filter or discrimination (pages 12, 15).

But Frederick Leboyer doesn't just explain the newborn's pain; he also talks about possible solutions. He advises giving birth in relatively quiet surroundings, picking the child up gently, and letting the umbilical cord finish pulsating before it's severed. The idea is to prevent, if possible, the child from first experiencing life as a desperate struggle for breath. Leboyer's goal is to allow the child to enter this alien world of gravity, light, and strange sounds slowly. And the pulsing umbilical cord allows for a more gradual transition.

After all, a child's first experiences and impressions of this world may influence it for life.

This book has changed me. Hans and I have new goals for this birth, and we want to find a doctor who will listen to us.

August 30
When I went to the doctor for a prenatal visit, Damaris and Miriam waited at the door for my return. When I came in, they stormed over, yelling, "Mommy, Mommy, where's our baby?" They know that the doctor has something to do with the child's birth. I've told them about labor and delivery over and over—they can't hear it often enough. And they want me to tell about each of their own births, way back then. They're learning the connections between sex and birth very naturally. Today three-year-old Miriam gave me some sex education. She related her childish impressions joyfully, ending with a sign, "I wish we could look in and see it!"

The bassinet with its little down covering is suffering from overload. Since we've had it in the apartment, the children have filled it with their favorite toys for the new little brother or sister.

The other night when I called Hans for dinner he didn't answer. So I went up to his study on the top floor to look for him. Where did I find him? In an armchair, buried in a textbook on midwifery. He didn't even hear me come in!

We acquired a new dream: we want to experience this birth at home. I could imagine it so vividly: Hans at my side, or even helping the doctor or nurse; our newborn child remaining close to us in the room; the joy of the other children.

Our family practitioner didn't agree, and he dutifully recited all the risks. But I cheerfully worked on him, and began to shape up our home "delivery room." We filled it with the needed bed, cloths, blankets, basins, and joyful anticipation—only our little one was missing.

But today the X-rays showed that the baby will probably be born in breech position. We'll have to go to the clinic after all, because of all the risks to the child. I'm depressed about that—I was so excited about having my child close to me from the very first hour. I wanted to give it a special sense of home and security. So much for that plan. Hans comforts me with the reminder that he'll still be with me during the birth.

And Dr. Centner is the understanding physician we've always looked for. When we asked if my husband could be present at the birth, he said, "Well, I was present at the births of my six children; so why should I hinder other men from being with their wives during those special hours?"

And, once more, God has provided someone to help me at home. Margaret is done with school, but she wants to get some practical experience with children before starting her studies in education. So we again have an older daughter for a year. She'll be a big help now that I'm having the baby in the hospital, and we live together as one big, happy family.

September 5
Reuben's birth: Saturday night, my water bag broke prematurely, so I was losing all the amniotic fluid. They took me to the clinic flat on my back in an ambulance. Hans faithfully rode along with me, although I hardly had any contractions. The nurses wanted to send him home, since it didn't look like the birth would be anytime soon; but he planted himself in the chair next to my bed, and prepared to stick the night out with me. He was so tired he kept nodding off, but I couldn't sleep. The contractions began to come at shorter intervals, yet they seemed bearable to me. I kept my eyes on my husband's face. It was wonderful just to have him with me, and to know that he would allow me—no, he *wanted* me—to wake him whenever I needed him. What security!

When the nurse came in to check me, Hans asked her how much longer she thought the birth would take. I was a bit annoyed—it seemed to me that the actual birth was a long way off. To my surprise, the nurse answered, "You should have your child by tomorrow morning." It was 2 A.M. I felt alert, in spite of my lack of sleep. They wheeled me into the delivery room at 3:40. I could feel the child within me, and I knew he was being pushed and squeezed together with every contraction. "I'll make myself very wide for you," I addressed the little one inwardly. "You won't have to endure this pain for very long." Just then I clearly felt the child sliding along the pelvic floor. "The baby is coming," I said. The doctor started to put on his sterile gloves, but he only had one on when the little foot and rear of our son appeared.

"May I make a request?" I asked quickly. "If everything goes well, and the child seems healthy, would you please turn off those harsh beams and leave only soft lights on? And also—would you let the umbilical cord finish pulsating, and lay my little one on my belly just as it is?" The doctor grinned and agreed to everything.

The birth was unbelievably fast: our child was born at 4:08 A.M. They turned the bright lights off, and I looked at my baby in a soft light. He only cried once or twice. Then I felt his small, warm body, which had lived inside me for nine months, lying on my belly all new and untouched. A thousand suns, whose warmth I could hardly bear, burst within me. I was still gripping my husband's hand, and he lovingly laid his arm over me and the child. We hadn't even spoken to each other during the birth—in fact, I wasn't clearly aware of his presence during the last phase of labor. But he was like a screen of protection around me, helping this new life begin in peace.

Shortly before the birth, Hans had read to me from his opened Bible: " 'I,' declares the Lord, 'will be a wall of fire around her, and I will be the glory in her midst' " (Zechariah 2:5). My husband had prayed that this glory would come down to me. And we had experienced that secure wall of love. We've learned something new and amazing about grace.

September 7
My dearest husband,

If I didn't have you, the value of every birth would be hidden from me, like lost treasure. I would have only inklings of these wonderful pearls—these pearls which must be ardently searched for. I deliberately set out to find them, and I rejoiced in the beauty of each new discovery. Altogether, I've found five pearls; each one ripening for its day of revelation, safe in the mussel's shell and the depths of the sea.

And today we both saw and felt and admired the perfection of our smallest pearl—for the first time we saw him in the light. It's so exciting! Every pearl makes me long for the next, because I'm discovering that each one is uniquely special. Are you starting to suspect that I'm strongly attached to these pearls? Well, look at the earlier ones: our little whirlwind Miriam, with her enchanting charm and her unsurpassed cheekiness; our loving Damaris, who likes to give gifts and spread joy; our Esther, growing up so fast and already such a pretty little person; our Mark, a rascal with a very fine spirit. And now our youngest pearl, the one with the velvet skin and black downy head!

Today I'm giving back to you what you gave me in an intimate hour of love. For nine months the two of us, you and I, were united in me. Now a new person has come out of that union; untouched and fresh, he's entered this world to make a way for himself. But everywhere he goes, he will provide an unconscious demonstration of our unity. And we'll have the privilege of leading him through joy and sorrow.

Our path will also lead through joy and sorrow; but we belong together, and we'll travel together all the way. Today you held me tightly as I passed through the depths—what security your loving hands passed on to me! And then, just when the deep seemed about to give way to the infinite, the pearl appeared. You were there for that, too. We experienced those first moments of discovery together; and we kissed in unbearable joy over our newest little treasure.

Darling, I can't describe my joy in having you. I hope that it's obvious, every single day, how happy you make me!

Your rich wife

September 9
My lovely wife,

Our youngest fine specimen is four days old now, and I'm delighted with our little Reuben. But you make me happier than anything!

Again, I have to express my admiration: You were so marvelous at this birth! Not a cry, not a grimace of pain, not even a little moan! I, a bystander who could only give birth passively, was impressed by your royal attitude toward the whole process of birth. The labor didn't determine or influence *you*—but *you* held all the reins in your hands and you directed the birth. I think that's the goal which a woman giving birth should strive for; then the process of labor will not overcome her. It's not something that she undergoes or endures passively, because she stands over it. From a high plane she controls the process of birth, giving it an appropriate character. You were so wonderful!

I want to thank you for this whole experience; it's made a deep impression on me. Loving kisses to you,
Your happy husband

September 26
For nine months you slumbered inside me, you sweet little creature. Now you're lying next to me in bed, satiated with my milk; I'm admiring your little face, with its snub nose, round eyes, and tiny mouth.

Those last few weeks, I could hardly wait to hold you in my arms. Did you know, you're the fulfillment of my dearest, deepest childhood desires? I used to hold my dolls in my arms and fervently long that they'd come to life. And here you are, you little live doll! But you're more beautiful and precious than I could have imagined. And you're growing already—you're going to talk and run, laugh and cry, complain and rejoice. I have the privilege of guiding you through all that; but first I get to nurse you. I'd love to do that all day long, without interruption! That's because you still seem like a part of me. If I leave the house for a short time, or put you in another room, I feel lonely; it's like we're still one being, and only complete when we're together. And that's true, after all: you need my milk and care ... and I need you, my little one. What would I do with all this excess of love that floods my heart, without you? There's plenty of love to go around to all who need it: my husband and all our other children. Each child becomes a strong branch on the family tree, enriching us, uniting us, and giving us gifts. And every branch invigorates the others, giving us more room to grow.

It's hard for me to realize that one of these days you'll be walking. At the very moment of birth you began to separate yourself from me. First the umbilical cord, previously so vital, was severed; soon you will no longer need my milk; then one of these days you'll have learned to walk, and you won't even ask my hand for help. And yet—you'll remain my child till a ripe old age! I'm boundlessly happy about that.

November 5
I'm taking part in a conference in Austria; it's especially for nursing mothers and their children. I'm pleased with the openness with which we're discussing problems and swapping experiences. It all sounds so familiar: I've gone through so many of the same things! And

I'm so thankful for all those experiences, now, even the painful ones. They've allowed me to become intimately acquainted with myself.

And more and more I'm learning to live with my limits—of course, the limits themselves constantly change! My children widen them again and again. And the boundaries I do feel don't discourage me, because they delineate for me the space in which I can move freely. Once I know them, I don't have to bump into them all the time. Being without limits isn't my goal, anyway; I'm much more interested in learning to use the freedom I do have. My eyes are being opened to the options inside the fence. Maybe I can't fulfill dreams of the footloose and fancy-free life—voyages around the world, all the beautiful furniture I would like and the latest fashions on my back. But I don't regret all that, because I appreciate what I have instead: my family and the security of God's love, which lets me live in peace with myself, my husband and my children.

November 15
Today Reuben cried horribly, and I was simply at a loss. Changing him didn't do anything, carrying him around didn't quiet him down, and even offering him my breast, which usually has a calming effect, didn't seem to help at all. He was completely beside himself, as if something terrible had happened. It upset me badly to feel so helpless. Finally, I lay on my side and

put the screaming bundle in the crook of my pulled-up legs. His head was right next to my abdomen. Hardly knowing why I was doing it, I began to breathe deeply, with the abdominal breathing I had practiced when I was pregnant. After a few breaths, the crying faded away. The little person seemed to be trying to recapture a memory, as though something familiar from the past had reminded him of a nice experience. Sometimes he would stop breathing for an instant, and his facial muscles relaxed so that it almost looked as if he were smiling. I felt that watching his face allowed me to look into his little soul. I tried to follow my child into a dark world of hollows—a unique experience of which I could only grasp a shadow. But the shadow was sufficient to give me a deep joy; and it also awoke a longing in my heart to experience that world for myself.

A new dimension of my humanity has opened up to me: that period of becoming in the enclosure of the uterus. In my mind it corresponds to the bliss of total security; it's like a warm summer night when I sit at the open window and watch the moonlight falling on the silhouettes of the mountains. I'm relaxing in a soft rocking chair, and from far away I hear the music of one of the old masters—Beethoven, Mozart, or perhaps Tchaikovsky. No one demands anything of me; I have no responsibilities or desires. I breathe because it feels good. I'm alive because living is enjoyable. It's the dusk time of life: No one forces me to sleep, and no one wants me to wake up. Is this dream a reality, or is reality a dream? My body doesn't feel like a body to me. It doesn't encumber me—it's as light as a butterfly's wings. I move with the weightlessness of a swimmer who glides unhurriedly through the depths of a mountain lake.

The rocking chair doesn't enclose me tightly; rather, it acts as a cloak to protect me, warm me, shield me from violence, fear, and death. Even this thought slumbers inside me, as a premonition and not a conscious understanding.

Moments like this are gems, flashing tiny reflections of what Heaven must be like. This is the true life for which I long. I understand the yearning of our existence for a life which is beyond this one.

December 8
I was asked to give a talk on the question "How can one serve God through one's children?" It always gives me great joy to speak on the cares and strains, and the positive responses and fulfillment, of motherhood.

It touched me to hear another mother of five children say, "I used to feel terrible guilt because of my impatience with the children. Over and over I despaired because my as yet unborn children were often in conflict with my own desires. Even after they're born, I don't always have a 'yes' in my heart toward them. But it's comforting to know that I'm not the only one to experience this; I don't have to be perfect in order to be a good mother. It *is* possible to make mistakes without damaging my children. I need to learn to have a 'yes' to myself, even toward my faults; I don't have to push them aside, because it's possible to overcome them bit by bit. And that will help me be a better mother. Acceptance and readiness to forgive will be the fundamentals I cling to from now on, and starting today I'll put them on a sign and hang them in my kitchen."

January 6
Today is our tenth anniversay—Where have the years gone?

It's all as vivid as yesterday: the ringing of the bells echoes in my ears, and I see the beaming wedding guests and hear Aunt Hildegard playing the anthem. My heart skips a beat when I remember Hans coming through the door to pick me up for the wedding. In church I sang the hymn with all my heart—"Praise to the Lord, the Almighty, the King of Creation"—but Hans listened very quietly, too excited to sing.

We've been given five children since then. Our love has changed. The exuberance of being in love has deepened into the consciousness of true security; the storms of youthful infatuation have changed into complete affirmation of the other; and the waves of misunderstanding have been smoothed by the decision to fully forgive and accept the loved one. I'm so thankful for these ten years! And I'm grateful for our children who, while passing through their own childhood, continually teach us to remain flexible.

January 10
My child is awakening into personality, as from a deep sleep. He's beginning to unfold and spread his wings like a butterfly. Till now my love surrounded him; but the purity of his own happiness radiates back to me from his smiling mouth today. He catches my joy and returns it to me like a mirror. I wish I could gaze into his pure, clean mirror all the time!

Every child brings me a fresh start; my children keep me young. Each birth changes me by making me open to the new and capable of reflecting on the old.

In order to claim my child, I have to meet him at his level. Doing this takes me straight back into my own childhood. Old images come alive: Why not let myself soar in the air on a swing, once more? Why not go down the slide with my smallest child, when he's afraid to go alone? I have no time to find answers to these "Why nots"—so I play and enjoy life with my family. There's no room in my life for complacency, boredom, or even conceit. I've once more become a questioner and a seeker; for my children always want to know something about eternity, or Heaven, or the size of the stars and the universe... or why they weren't invited to our wedding, or whether an earthworm has teeth.

February 5
It's evening. Our apartment is lit by twilight, and the wonderful hour of play has begun: The game? Hide! Turning on the light isn't permitted. One person counts, and before you know it everyone's disappeared. Daddy crawls under the bed, Mommy stands behind the curtain with the baby, Miriam crouches in back of the door, Mark squats behind the armchair. Everywhere you look there's a little screamer sitting silent as a mouse. What breathtaking peace! It only lasts until the first hider is found, with a shout of "Hey!" One by one, we're all coaxed out of hiding. The apartment looks like a disheveled haystack—but what a happy place! You want to hide yourself from the others so that you can rediscover each one, and be amazed once again over how many people surround you. The joy of having, knowing, and belonging to one another continues to grow. What wealth we have in each other!

My child,

Your existence touches my heart like a sunrise, or like a wind caresses the quaking grass. You fill me with joy! Sometimes my soul swings on the highest branches of the firs; it swoops up into the heavens like skylark, it sings like a delicate flute, it bounds across the mountains with the grace of a deer, it bubbles like the clear crystal spring in the valley.

Who can grasp the wealth of this existence? Wide, free, soft, tender, happy, peaceful: I hold a piece of

Chapter Five

Heaven in my arms. Dear child, what a rich blessing you are.

Your existence raises me above everyday trials, above agitation, above indifference, above meaninglessness. You belong with me, as I belong with you. But you don't belong *to* me—you've been entrusted to me as a fief from God. We will work together on each other, so that our Lord can find delight in us when he returns.

I never tire of examining you in wonder. What a craftmaster is the one who made you! You give me stupendous glimpses of his greatness. And if he created you in me, doesn't he have the power to order all things in my life?

January 1978
When Mark came home from school today, I could tell that something was bothering him. He kept watching me with a question in his eyes, but it took him a long time to express it. Finally he blurted out, "Mommy, are we rich? Martin says he can't be my friend unless we're rich." We sat down at the table together.

"What does it mean to be rich?" I asked him.

"It means you have a lot of money," he answered promptly.

"But you can also be rich in other things. Being rich simply means that you've got a lot of a certain thing."

"Then I'm rich, because I have lots of cars!" he

said excitedly. "And you," he added slowly, "you're rich too, because you have all of us!" Happily Mark jumped up from his chair and ran into the children's room. I could hear him singing his newfound song, up and down the scale: "We are rich, we are rich, we are rich . . ."

And in my heart I rejoiced with him: "Yes, we are so rich!"